Preservation

By the same author

Fiction

THE DEADWEIGHT
NOW OR NEVER
STILL ALIVE TOMORROW

Non-fiction

THE ITALIAN LEFT
THE MONTESI SCANDAL
EROS DENIED

With Elizabeth Young

OLD LONDON CHURCHES

WAYLAND KENNET

Preservation

TEMPLE SMITH · LONDON

First published in Great Britain 1972
by Maurice Temple Smith Ltd
37 Great Russell Street, London WC1
Copyright © 1972 Wayland Kennet
ISBN 0 8511 7022 6
Printed in Great Britain by
The Redwood Press, Trowbridge

Acknowledgments

I thank Miss Jan Parry for research help for Chapter I and for the index; Mr Hugh Crallan, Mr Stephen Weeks, Mrs Arbuthnot-Lane, Mr Stanley Edgcumbe, and Mr David Roberts and Mr Geoffrey Clarke of Cambridge, for providing material for Chapter IV.

I thank also my wife for being a tuning fork, and Mrs Judith Beetham for the typing.

The illustrations are reproduced by kind permission, as follows:

National Monuments Record: 1, 5, 6; *Bath Evening Chronicle*: 2, 3; Stephen Weeks: 4; Tom Molland Ltd: 9; Sotheby & Co: 10; Edward Leigh: 11, 12, 13, 15; *Architectural Review*: 14.

Contents

Illustrations

I

Some history

The first European building to be preserved by law was the Colosseum. That is not surprising; we marvel that people should so long ago have been able to build anything so vast. Some go on to think of the history of engineering, and how very long it was before another concrete building of anything like that size was achieved. Others think of the history of architecture, and how the Colosseum has written on its face the three stages of Greek dendromorphism: the bare tree-trunk of the Doric, the furled fern of the Ionic, and the profuse acanthus of the Corinthian. Others again think of the gladiators and the lions, *morturi te salutant*, the Christians torn and eaten, the Emperor giving Thumbs Down, the Vestal Virgins, the naval battles, and the wooden Christian cross which has now laid all these ghosts. We see the Colosseum both as architecture and as history.

The Colonna and Frangipani families did not; they saw it as a mountain. For most of the middle ages the chief diversion of the Roman and Latin nobles, and the chief misery of the Roman and Latin people, was the war between the Colonna and Orsini clans. For much of that time the Frangipani of the Colonna faction, and their troops, lived in the Colosseum, while the Orsini and their troops lived in various other ruins round the city. The Frangipani walled up parts of the great Roman passages and tunnels, lit fires, and knocked other parts down to let the light in. During the few years of peace

11

they carried away convenient pieces of marble to make themselves houses and palaces elsewhere, with tall towers from which to look down on other clans. In course of time, many others followed their example.

At some point certain people began to think—'This must stop; the Colosseum ought to be preserved.' It is impossible to discover just when this happened. Perhaps it was even before the Orsinis and Colonnas began their feud. In 546 Belisarius explained to the Ostrogothic invader, Totila, that if he was going to take Rome, he might as well refrain from destroying it first. But they were still destroying the Colosseum and the Orsini and Colonna were still fighting, when Brunelleschi came from Florence in 1405 to make measured drawings of the ruins of antiquity, a journey which was the beginning of the visual part of the Renaissance. Still in 1450 Nicholas V, otherwise reputed a cultivated pontiff, is supposed to have removed two thousand cartloads of marble from the Colosseum in a single year. Fifty years after that, the Borgia Pope Alexander VI simply leased it out on normal terms for exploitation as a commercial quarry. By 1520 Giulio Romano was painting the first pictures ever deliberately to use ruins for emotional effect. This was perhaps the beginning of the picturesque approach to conservation; if something moves people, they are bound to want to keep it.

But it was not until the middle of the eighteenth century that Pope Benedict XIV declared the Colosseum sacred to the Passion of Christ, because of the early Christians killed there, and forbade anyone to carry away any more of it. Benedict XIV was not only the first ruler to preserve by law, he was also, as one would expect, a good Pope; he earned the respect of Hume, Montesquieu, and even Voltaire. Horace Walpole wrote of him: 'He was loved by Papists, esteemed by Protestants, a Priest without insolence or interest, a Prince without favourites, a Pope without nephews.' The Colosseum is still there to amaze, to over-awe, even to appal, and there is surely no-one who will question the rightness of Benedict XIV's action, and few who will not wonder that a millennium and a half passed before it was taken.

When we seek to preserve an ancient building, which would otherwise fall or be demolished, we seek to preserve an evidence, an example, and an emblem.

An ancient building is evidence of the way our ancestors lived, which must become more and more interesting to us as we become more and more aware that the end of our way of life is in sight. We cannot continue for ever to become richer and more numerous; the time will come when we must limit both population growth and economic growth as we now understand it. Our ancestors were poorer and less numerous, and the way they lived is yearly becoming more important to us. We do not have to ascribe virtue to them to be fascinated; it is enough to establish their ecological moderation. In their dwellings and places of assembly we trace the origins of our own institutions. Eton is not a comprehensive school, but comprehensive schools derive from it; polytechnics derive from Oxford, municipal parks from Stowe and Stourhead, blocks of flats from Edinburgh High Street, and the semi detached house we now love best derives via Voysey from fifteenth-century farmhouses. It is the same with our political institutions: we are governed by a Parliament, consisting of Lords and Commons. When it was first set up, the Lords lived in castles and the burgesses lived in medieval town centres; plenty of both survive.[1] We have clergymen: they were not always what they are now, and we can also see that in stone and brick.

These things not only become more interesting to those who are interested in them, they also interest more

---

[1] What is said to be the first portrait of a member of the House of Commons is at Great Chalfield Manor in Wiltshire: late fifteenth century.

people. In our fathers' time, only the better off could afford to travel to look at them or buy the books which described them. They alone had the education to trace the historical links. Now all of us can.

A fine building preserved is also commonly an example of a class of beautiful things. If there were only one medieval cathedral in England instead of twenty, we should be less than a twentieth as lucky. We would not know that such a thing could ever be repeated, and it is the prodigality and ubiquity of good, whether of beauty or virtue or wit, which is humanity's chief ground for hope. To carry a category in our minds is reassuring; to know we can find another example of it, and that one our own one, round the corner, roots us and even defines us. All fine buildings preserved are examples of the over-arching category: fine buildings. What is a beautiful building? Well, what is a beautiful man or woman? Mainly, one who resembles other beautiful men and women; one who deviates least from that comforting excellence of form and colour and texture and proportion which we have grown up with, and which we agree to call beautiful. Also one whom it would be delightful to embrace. The same with a building: one which in its kind—as norman, perpendicular, renaissance, baroque, palladian, gothick—deviates least from the familiar and median without yet boring us; also one which it would be delightful to live in. Without beautiful buildings we would no longer be sure what beautiful buildings were, and we should find it hard to build any.

A fine building preserved is also an emblem of our attachment to values more pleasant and joyful than money. To say 'preserve' is to say 'spend', or 'exert' or 'forgo profit'. At least here, we say, at least this once, we will do something interesting, difficult, and altruistic. Tomorrow, or over there, we will resume the grey treadmill: but let this stand. It is the gentler and more solicitous side of us bodied forth in old stone or brick. We smile at each other when we see it, thinking how much nicer it is than what would have replaced it, and how much nicer we are than the people who wanted to knock it down. And lastly, some buildings are eagles' feathers: we shall never 'see Shelley plain', but we can see where he lived, and we shall want to keep the memory on our inner mantlepiece. Others will keep the memory not of a dead poet, but of a live duke.

An evidence, an example, and an emblem. Yes, but often a bit of kindly commonsense too. An existing house, or street, or quarter is usually a going concern. But this does not mean that the land on which it stands might not be used more profitably. Our society is based, and always has been, on the assumption that citizens may pursue profit unless and until they look like hurting other citizens. Is breaking up a local community which is a going concern 'hurting other citizens'? It very often is, and when that is so there is no reason why profit should have the day. It would not perhaps be a crime to knock down the quarter and begin again; but it might well be a waste of national resources for the profit of the few. There are enough undoubted slums to keep the building industry occupied, and preservation often means preservation of a loved way of life, as well as of interesting buildings.

Let us turn now to the history of preservation in England, and to the way in which our present system of law and practice grew up.

The three safest ways of preventing old buildings being pulled down are, in order, gaining direct control of them, by ownership or otherwise; making the owner ashamed of wanting to pull them down, and having laws saying they may not be pulled down. We may call these ways the Aubrey, the Stukeley and the Lubbock.

Countless civilised noblemen and other men of means have since the beginning of architecture, owned fine buildings and taken good care of them. But let us take John Aubrey as the patron saint of manœuvring yourself into a position where you can control the fate of an old building you admire. Though he had the same tutor at Malmesbury as Hobbes, he turned out less monolithic. For him, the common weal was indeed the sum of each individual weal, but how much more interesting were all the individual weals. To read him is to be guaranteed never a moment's boredom by generalisation. He liked the bells of Broadchalke church, and the church itself, and maintains that if he and another Wiltshire worthy had not got themselves made churchwardens 'the fair church had fallen, from the niggardliness of the church-wardens of mean condition'. That is the direct approach, the do-it-yourself. It is still not sufficiently practised. Niggardly stewards are as prevalent now as they were in the seventeenth century.

William Stukeley, an eighteenth-century clergyman who held that the Bacchus of the poets was none other than Jehovah in different guise, and that the name of Hackpen Hill in Wiltshire was derived from Parnassus,[1] was also the first researcher into Avebury and Silbury, which are in their way as impressive as the Pyramids and, the most recent research suggests, probably about the same age. He coined the phrase which can well preside over all polemics for preservation and diatribes against developers: he lamented how a farmer of Avebury broke up the stones of the sanctuary on Seven Barrow Hill, of which none now remain, 'for the little, dirty profit'. We will take him as the patron saint of shaming, of the appeal to the owner's better nature. And Sir John Lubbock, first Lord Avebury, whose part in introducing preservation law into England we will shortly examine, shall serve us as onomastic for the final recourse which a society has; to law.[2]

[1]William Stukeley, *Abury, a Temple of the British Druids*, 1743, p. 67.
[2]It may be due to unconscious campanilism on my part, though I do not think so, that all three of my prototype episodes are drawn from Wiltshire, and that two of them are connected with

The power to preserve buildings of historic interest was only taken by states after almost a century of discussion and polemic about the best way to restore them. This polemic was often extremely violent. In England it was perhaps James Wyatt whose bold way with an old building started the whole movement for preservation and for the respect of historical reality in architecture. Between 1770 and his death in 1813 he went through a good many of the castles and cathedrals of England shortening them where convenient, rebuilding the West fronts, altering East ends, switching reredoses and organs, building up keeps and battlements. Lichfield, Salisbury, Hereford, Westminster were seen to by him, and always hot on his heels in the columns of the *Gentleman's Magazine* came his contemporary John Carter, correcting, blaming, scourging. Wyatt never replied.

At last, in 1796, Carter caught up with him at Durham. Wyatt had already got as far as rebuilding the East front, taking out the stained glass, adding the present North Porch, rebuilding the turrets of the Eastern transept to his own design, and pulling down the entire Norman chapter house. But at that point John Carter, mobilising the Society of Antiquaries, stopped him in his tracks before he could demolish Bishop Hatfield's tomb and throne and Bishop Neville's reredos, or add an octagonal lantern and tall spire, or demolish the great Norman Galilee Chapel at the East end in order to make room for a carriage drive.

The history of the ecclesiological movement, of the

Avebury itself. The antiquities of Wiltshire are so impressive, the fact that the county is now probably less populous than it was five thousand years ago is so extraordinary, and Avebury, perhaps even more than Stonehenge, is so gigantic and so awe-inspiring that it is only natural that English preservationism should have begun and developed here. I say ' here ' because this is written more or less in the shadow of Avebury and because the river from which I take my name rises at Avebury.

Camden Society, of the Pugins, and of Sir Gilbert Scott, is well-known and, as far as they contributed to the growth of the public opinion which made possible and necessary the first state controls, can perhaps be summarised thus: Wyatt's cavalier surgery begot Pugin's and Ruskin's passionate advocacies, as much liturgical as architectural. They held not that the medieval was good because it was beautiful, but that it was beautiful because it was good; that is, it expressed the most godly kind of worship. Pugin in turn begot Sir Gilbert Scott and his immense one-man industry of correct restoration and correct new Gothic churches. And it was Sir Gilbert Scott, by his work at Tewkesbury Abbey in particular, who drove William Morris, the printer and designer, and would-be restorer of guild-socialism, to found the Society for the Protection of Ancient Buildings in 1877. This was the first pressure group for preservation as we know pressure groups in the modern age.

Morris's action was to the care of old buildings in the nineteenth century what Queen Elizabeth's Settlement was to the history of the church in the sixteenth; he stopped the pendulum. He saw that if generation after generation went on adjusting the old buildings to conform to their own idea of the beauty or piety of antiquity, there would soon be nothing left. The only reasonable thing to do was to take them as they were, accretion, patching and all, and keep them that way. 'Scrape' had given rise to 'anti-scrape'. The Society of Antiquaries, though its main concerns were for the written records, the heraldry, and the movable objects, had indeed stopped Wyatt at Durham. But it had been founded as a learned coterie and had never considered itself as a pressure group. There was now a need for precisely that.

Here is part of William Morris's foundation manifesto for the Society for the Protection of Ancient Buildings:

A Society coming before the public with such a name as

that above written must needs explain how, and why, it proposes to protect those ancient buildings which, to most people, doubtless, seem to have so many and such excellent protectors. This, then, is the explanation we offer.

No doubt within the last fifty years a new interest, almost like another sense, has arisen in these ancient monuments of art; and they have become the subject of one of the most interesting of studies, and of an enthusiasm, religious, historical, artistic, which is one of the undoubted gains of our time; yet we think that if the present treatment of them be continued, our descendants will find them useless for study and chilling to enthusiasm. We think that those last fifty years of knowledge and attention have done more for their destruction than all the foregoing centuries of revolution, violence and contempt.

For Architecture, long decaying, died out, as a popular art at least, just as the knowledge of mediaeval art was born. So that the civilized world of the nineteenth century has no style of its own amidst its wide knowledge of the styles of other centuries. From this lack and this gain arose in men's minds the strange idea of the Restoration of ancient buildings; and a strange and most fatal idea, which by its very name implies that it is possible to strip from a building this, that, and the other part of its history—of its life that is—and then to stay the hand at some arbitrary point, and leave it still historical, living, and even as it once was.

In early times this kind of forgery was impossible, because knowledge failed the builders, or perhaps because instinct held them back. If repairs were needed, if ambition or piety pricked on to change, that change was of necessity wrought in the unmistakable fashion of the time; a church of the eleventh century might be added to or altered in the twelfth, thirteenth, fourteenth, fifteenth, sixteenth, or even the seventeenth or eighteenth centuries; but every change, whatever history it destroyed, left history in the gap. . .

For what is left we plead before our architects themselves, before the official guardians of buildings, and before the public generally, and we pray them to remember how much is gone of the religion, thought and manners of time past, never by almost universal consent to be restored; and to consider whether it be possible to restore those buildings, the living spirit of which, it cannot be too often repeated, was an inseparable part of that religion and thought and those past manners. For our part we assure them fearlessly, that of all the restorations yet undertaken the worst have meant the reckless stripping a building of some of its most interesting material features; while the best have their exact analogy in the restoration of an old picture, where the partly perished work of the ancient craftsmaster has been made neat and smooth by the tricky hand of some unoriginal and thoughtless hack of today. If, for the rest, it be asked us to specify what kind or amount of art, style, or other interest in a building, makes it worth protecting, we answer, anything which can be looked on as artistic, picturesque, historical, antique, or substantial: any work, in short, over which educated, artistic people would think it worth while to argue at all.

It is for all these buildings, therefore, of all times and styles, that we plead, and call upon those who have to deal with them to put Protection in the place of Restoration, to stave off decay by daily care, to prop a perilous wall or mend a leaky roof by such means as are obviously meant for support or covering, and show no pretence of other art, and otherwise to resist all tampering with either the fabric or ornament of the building as it stands. . .

Morris was in no doubt what the ancient buildings needed protecting against: false protectors like Sir Gilbert Scott. The SPAB was attended by the success which customarily attended William Morris's enterprises, and is still very much alive. It is the first preservation society in England, the direct parent of the Georgian Group, thus the direct grandparent of the Victorian Society, and perhaps the indirect progenitor of all the preservation societies there are in our country.

The foundation of the SPAB coincided in time with the first attempts to legislate in England. The history of state preservation of the architectural heritage of Europe begins, like the history of most other state activities before 1917, in France, to which we must now briefly turn. After the 1830 Revolution, the Guizot government decided to publish the 'unpublished documents of French history'. These were to include not only documents as such, but also the making and publication of a complete documentation on all the historic monuments which had ever existed in France: *une véritable statistique monumentale*. This chacteristically encyclopedic approach had to undergo various refinements before it could issue into the realm of the possible. In 1835 there was set up a *Comité des Lettres, Philosophies, Sciences, et Arts,* which included among others Victor Hugo and the founder of modern preservationism, Prosper Mérimée. The terms of reference were indeed rather broad for any useful purpose, and Mérimée complained in a letter that nothing was done: 'Victor Hugo just gives us poetry about everything'.

By 1837 a *Comité Spécial des Arts et Monuments* was hived off which was to draw up an inventory and preserve threatened ruins and buildings. Mérimée reckoned its work as planned would take 200 years and result in 900 volumes; he called it 'naive administrative romanticism'. He succeeded in cutting the operation down to a workable size, and by 1840 had secured a list of fifty-nine monuments, and a minute state budget of 105,000 francs to help keep them standing. These were the first 'list' and the first state funds in European history. In 1841 the law was extended to permit the state compulsorily to purchase monuments which were being neglected, but not enough money was voted to allow this to have any significant effect. It was not until 1887 that the French State took power to forbid the destruction of a listed building, though even here its power to enforce the sanction rested at the end of the day on its willingness to compensate the owner for the financial loss that preservation might impose upon him.

The first British attempts to legislate stemmed from the determination of Sir John Lubbock, first Lord Avebury, to whose remarkable career, as the founder of our present system, we must now turn. He left Eton at fourteen, and went straight into the family bank; but a curtailed education did not stop him becoming Vice-Chancellor of the University of London, President of the Anthropological Society, Chairman of the London County Council, inventor of Bank Holidays (called at first St Lubbock's Day) and of Early Closing. He was also a prolific and original writer on entomology, anthropology, archaeology, scenery, and the history of literature. As Darwin wrote to him in 1882: 'How on earth you find the time is a mystery to me.' His second wife was the daughter of General Pitt Rivers, the doyen of Victorian archaeology.

In 1872 the Reverend Bryan King, Rector of Avebury,[1] telegraphed to Lubbock that part of the Circle had been 'sold to a land company which resold it in small building lots for the erection of cottages', and that construction was to begin the following Monday. But the cottages were not too happy, and would sell for a guinea each. Lubbock telegraphed to King to give them their guineas, and thus bought the threatened land. Later he also bought Silbury Hill and West Kennet Farm, including the West Kennet long barrow and Hackpen Hill.[2] It was from Avebury that he later took the name of his peerage.

In 1873, when the history of preservation law in England begins, Lubbock was Liberal member of parliament for Maidstone. He introduced his National Monuments Preservation Bill into the House of Commons in vain every year from 1873 to 1879. It proposed to set up a National Monuments Commission, consisting of the Presidents of the societies of Antiquaries of England, Scotland and London, of the Royal Irish Academy, the Keeper of British Antiquities at the British Museum, the Master of the Rolls, and so on. There would be a schedule of monuments, meaning mounds, tumuli,

[1] For more about whom, see *Old London Churches* by Wayland and Elizabeth Young, Faber, 1956, p. 289.
[2] *The Life of Sir John Lubbock,* Horace G. Hutchinson, London 1914; p. 131.

barrows and dykes. They were expressly not to be ruined buildings, and even those mounds, etc. which formed part of castle or abbey ruins, or stood in anybody's park or garden, were also expressly excluded. In the case of a scheduled monument the Commission could, after giving the owner notice, assume a 'power of restraint'. Appeal lay to the courts against the notice. If the power of restraint were operative, and the owner then wanted to 'injure' the monument, he would have to serve a 'requisition' on the Commission, who were then compelled either to consent or to purchase the monument. The Commission could also acquire, by agreement with the owner, either the freehold, or the right of public access, or the 'power of restraint'. Once it owned the freehold, the Commission was expressly empowered to inspect or break open any monument. The Commission might spend money on restoring and preserving scheduled monuments, though only with the consent of the Treasury, and the same for compensation in respect of the acquisition of the 'right of restraint'. When vested in the Commission, monuments were to be de-rated.

We shall see later how much of our present preservation law is pre-figured in Lubbock's 1873 Bill, so it will be interesting to pause for a while to examine the reasons why Lubbock's proposals were resisted for forty years. His Bill reached substantive debate on the floor of the House of Commons for the first time in 1875. Lubbock said the main effect 'of the bill was really to gain a little time during which the nation or locality might, if so disposed, become the purchaser of such monuments'. He 'could not imagine that this House or the country could grudge a moderate sum to preserve our ancient monuments' but really believed that the expense to the country would be infinitesimally small. The amount would in any case be determined by the Treasury, subject to the approval of Parliament. 'It was one thing to keep up old houses which required endless repairs, and the monuments dealt with in this bill only wanted to be left alone.' Lubbock had heard it said that 'under the bill any man's house might be invaded by bands of destructive and enthusiastic antiquaries, that the Englishman's house would cease to be his castle, and so forth'. The truth of the matter was the bill could only affect a man 'whose lodging was on the cold ground', because it only applied to mounds and earthworks.

But this preliminary defence did not stop the property interests from setting up an Aunt Sally which bore little relation to the bill. Sir Charles Legard, a Tory baronet, thought that the bill, 'comprising an enormous area and concerning such extraordinary powers', should be a government one, not a private member's. It was 'a measure of spoliation . . . legalising burglary by daylight . . . invading the right of private property.' 'When a power of restraint in respect of a monument is vested in the Commissioners by agreement or purchase, they or any person authorised in writing by any of them may at any time between sunrise and sunset enter upon and inspect the monument and all parts thereof and may in case of necessity break open any door or enclosure preventing their access without being liable for any action or prosecution for trespass or otherwise.' . . . (This power was only proposed in respect of monuments owned by the Commission itself.) 'How will the philanthropic individuals who are to have power vested in them to perform these acts of violence and daring to be adequately rewarded?—Why they are to be remunerated out of the pockets of the people.' No less than sixteen barrows on his own property had been damaged by well-meaning friends digging them up and picnicking round them. 'The House could not tell where the ravages of mediaeval curiosity-mongers would stop . . . the tombs of our fore-fathers and ourselves would be neither safe nor sacred.' The bill was therefore 'an insult to the spirit and enterprise of private citizens who inherited these ancient monuments' and 'in no way conduced to the interests of an advanced and advancing civilisation.' Sir

Charles Legard's objection was based on the principle that the owners could be trusted to look after their own. He himself owned 6,500 acres in Yorkshire and was a hunting and shooting man.

Lord Francis Hervey, a Tory lawyer, went further: what was a 'national monument' anyway? Were the 'absurd relics' of our 'barbarian predecessors' who 'found time hanging heavily on their hands and set about piling up great barrows and rings of stones' really to be preserved, and that at the cost of infringement of property rights?

But other members claimed that Britain was lagging behind other countries and should proceed. Mr. Osborne Morgan, also a lawyer, said the objections 'appeared to him to spring from a respect of the rights of property run mad, for the bill treated private owners with the greatest tenderness.'

Mr W. H. Smith, Secretary to the Treasury, son of the founder of the firm, and known as 'Old Morality', answered for the Conservative Government. He said that he could never hope to submit an estimate of how much would be spent under the bill on ancient monuments; it would certainly be not hundreds but hundreds of thousands of pounds. Moreover, the proposed Commis sion would surely be strong enough to overcome legitimate government objections to the proposals it might make for public expenditure.

Answering the debate, Sir John Lubbock said it was 'for the House to determine whether it would exercise on behalf of the nation the right to preserve these monuments: whether it would maintain the right of individuals to destroy or the right of the nation to preserve.'

The bill passed neither that year nor in 1876.

In 1877 Lubbock introduced it again, simply saying that he had introduced it so often he would not detain the House with an account of what was in it. Lord Francis Hervey, whose views on the civilisation of his ancestors had now progressed to the point where he was able to describe its remains as 'destitute of all art and of everything that was noble or that entitled them to preservation', had also hit upon a new justification for eschewing statutory action. It was this: 'It is only when you have something not worth preserving that you have to fall back on the operation of the law.'

Mr Leighton, Chairman of the Shropshire Parish Register Society, speaking as an antiquarian, opposed the bill because it was insufficient in that it protected only certain monuments and not all. But 'the learned and voluntary societies should do this work and not the government.' People naturally felt a veneration for monuments in their neighbourhood and 'this patriotic and almost religious sentiment should be encouraged and intensified, but government ownership and official intervention would destroy it'. Preservation should therefore be left to local societies and private subscriptions, and at all costs one should steer clear of town councils. 'There was not a town in the country which did not bear witness to the bad taste of such bodies.'

Mr Grant Duff had been comparing Mr Leighton's and Lord Francis Hervey's speeches. It was indeed true that antiquities were best preserved by the interest which the masses of the people took in them, but 'how long will it take to get farm labourers to appreciate historic antiquities when an educated man like the Noble Lord holds them so cheap?' He was therefore in favour of the bill: it had no bearing on the rights of property; 'its only bearing is on the wrongs of property'.

The government (still the Conservative Government of Disraeli) this time put up the Attorney General, Sir John Holker, to shoot Lubbock down. He objected to the introduction into the law of the land of a principle that could have disastrous consequences: namely that of putting public interests above private rights. The most interesting passage of his speech was that in which he held up as thick ends of wedges, the thin ends of which were now before the House, a number of things which Parliament later did amid general acclamation. Why, he asked, should one stop at ancient remains? Why should one not also preserve medieval abbeys and castles? Why should one even stop there—why should one not impose restrictions on the owners of pictures or statues of great national interest? Was it not thinkable that one day there should be a demand that the owner of, say, Gainsborough's 'Blue Boy' be prevented from sending it out of the country? Yet further: if a circle of stones was worth preserving at the expense of an interference with private rights, could not the same be said for a row of beech trees? He feared that there was 'a growing desire on the part of honourable gentlemen opposite to make private rights subservient not only to public necessity but also to public convenience.'

Mr Cavendish Bentinck, a Conservative Member, 'did not pretend to be either an antiquary or a man of taste —he was particularly glad he was not a man of taste'. Mr Osborne Morgan was, though. Expenditure under the bill 'would not amount to one-tenth of the cost of an ironclad which went to the bottom of the sea and nobody said anything further about it.'

The Chancellor of the Exchequer, Sir Stafford Northcote, backed up the Attorney General with the same arguments which had been used from the Treasury bench two years earlier, and Lord Percy summed up the prevailing opinion in Parliament when he said that it was a proposal to take 'the property of owners not for utilitarian purposes, for railways and purposes of that sort, but for purposes of sentiment, and it was difficult to see where they would stop.' The bill was lost that year, and again in 1878 and 79.

In 1880 there was a general election: the Conservatives were defeated and Gladstone came back with a new Liberal government. Sir John Lubbock lost his seat against the swing because of a slum clearance in Maidstone which had been carried through without proper public consultation, and he could therefore no longer perform the annual rite in the House of Commons. Lord Percy, the great opponent, moved instead for a Select Committee to enquire into the 'number, situation and condition of ancient British, Celtic, Roman, Runic, Danish or Saxon monuments in the United Kingdom, of interest from a scientific, antiquarian or historical point of view, and to report what legislative measures (if any) are necessary for their preservation.' This transparent delaying device was not adopted; Lubbock's familiar bill had already, with the help of the Society of Antiquaries, listed the monuments to be preserved, so there was no need of a select committee. But equally it prevented the main proposal being considered that session.

In the same year, the House of Lords were for the first time seized of the matter. Lord Stanhope, gambling on a faint chance, said that since the House of Commons had got as far as amending and approving the bill in Committee (this had been the procedural high water mark, so far, in 1878) it ought to be taken up by the Lords. But too many peers owned the things in question for there to be any hope of their approving even the slight element of compulsion proposed. Lord De La Warr, Lord Redesdale, the Duke of Richmond; their gardens, their castles, their well known care for the heritage. . . . The proposal was dropped.

In 1881 Sir John Lubbock, having returned to the House of Commons as Member for London University, sought to involve the new Liberal Government in a general statement of neutrality at least. On a supply day he moved that 'it is desirable that the Government should take steps to provide for the protection of ancient monuments.' The formulation was general and innocuous, and Gladstone agreed, since the Government had no plans of its own, to consider any plan Lubbock might submit.

By then public opinion, in the wake of William Morris's Society for the Preservation of Ancient Buildings, was on the move, and Gladstone was not weighed down with the same property tail as the other party. It was in this new climate of opinion, and under a Liberal Government, that the first Ancient Monuments Protection Act was passed in 1882, and a poor thing it was. It differed from Sir John Lubbock's earlier proposal in leaving out any element of compulsion whatsoever, and this was all that was needed to get the foundation stone of our preservation system laid. It is always wise for a legislature, when it finds people are behaving badly but are not ready to admit it, to pass an act permitting them to behave well, to express astonishment that they do not avail themselves of this permission, and then, but only then, regretfully to pass another Act forbidding them to behave badly. Lubbock's mistake had been to omit the first step in the procedure.

The 1882 Bill was introduced into the House of Lords with a schedule of twenty-one ancient monuments, all stone circles (including Stonehenge), earthworks, and so on, 'as to the value of which', in the words of the Lord Chancellor 'there was an agreement among all persons interested in the preservation of ancient monuments.' The Bill itself simply said that the State might, if the owner agreed, purchase an ancient monument and look after it, or might take it into 'guardianship', which meant the owner remained owner but lost his power to demolish or remove it, in return for state aid in maintaining it. There was nothing to make the owner accept either of these arrangements if he did not want to: there was no trace now of Lubbock's proposal to give the Commission power to assume the 'right of restraint'.

Even so, there was too much conservation in the bill for the real Conservatives. Lord Salisbury himself, then Leader of the Opposition, moved an amendment to exclude from the schedule the property of his noble friend the Duke of Richmond, who had 'expressed himself as perfectly willing and able to protect the relic from destruction'. The amendment was negatived.

In the Commons the bill survived both the Tory attack (Mr Warton: 'invasion of the rights of property which is to be carried out under the bill in order to gratify the antiquarian tastes of a few at the public expense') and the mildly expressed regret of Sir John Lubbock himself that it did not go far enough. The Government was given powers to add 'similar' monuments to the schedule by Order in Council, and the bill passed.

Its passage was an instructive foretaste of things to come. The Liberals put it through. The Conservatives opposed it even in its weakest form; they opposed even giving help to such as might request it among the owners of twenty-nine scheduled monuments. Indeed within thirty years Lord Curzon, himself a high Tory if ever there was one, was saying[1]:

'It is almost incredible if one looks back at the Parliamentary history of the time' (1882) 'to find how much opposition was excited by that mild, inoffensive measure. . . This is a country in which the idea of property has always been more sedulously cherished than in any other, but when you see that to get that Bill through Parliament it had to be denuded of its important features and only after many years was it passed in an almost innocuous form into law, one feels almost ashamed of the reputation of one's countrymen.'

In 1900 Sir John Lubbock, having as we have seen purchased the stone circle at Avebury in order to pre- serve it, and taken the name of a peerage from it, had the pleasure of seeing the scope of the 1882 Act slightly widened. The 1900 Act allowed County Councils to pro- ceed in the same limited way as the 1882 Act had allowed central government to proceed (they never did), and established the principle of public access to Scheduled Ancient Monuments. But this Act also introduced a distinction which led to a needless duplication of administration and law in the period between 1944 and

[1]House of Lords debates on the 1912 bill; see p. 34.

1971. It is still doing so even now, after the amalgamation of the Ministry of Works and Ministry of Housing in the Department of the Environment. To qualify as an ancient monument a building or structure had to be uninhabited, or inhabited only by a caretaker. The idea was, of course, that if it was inhabited, so that it was actually somebody's home, it would be far too gross an infringement of property rights to allow central or local government to be among those to whom the owner might wish to sell it, or among those whose help he might seek in maintaining it. Uninhabited buildings were for eighty-eight years the responsibility of the Office, later Ministry, of Works and when inhabited buildings were brought in in the 1940s, it was another Minister who was made responsible.

In 1895 the National Trust had been founded. In its early days, it was concerned with open spaces; it actually came to birth because Canon Rawnsley, who loved the Lake District, and Sir Robert Hunter, Solicitor to the Post Office, who loved the Surrey Commons, met each other and Octavia Hill, who knew about setting up charities and getting good public relations. The principle of the National Trust was Aubrey's; if you love it, it is best to own it. So they began to acquire beautiful places, though it was many years before they acquired, any fine old houses, except in an incidental and unimportant fashion. In 1907 Parliament conferred on the National Trust the right of holding land 'inalienably'; that is to say, that nobody might acquire National Trust land without the leave of Parliament itself. This was forty years before compulsory purchase by public authorities became a normal instrument of social justice and economic progress and, when it did, the new provision had to respect the old. This fact has saved many precious places since 1945.

In 1908 the Royal Commission on Historical Monuments was set up, under the chairmanship of Lord Burghclere, to 'make an inventory of the Ancient and

Historical Monuments and Constructions connected with or illustrative of the contemporary culture, civilization and conditions of life of the people in England, excluding Monmouthshire, from the earliest times to the year 1700, and to specify those which seem most worthy of preservation.' It published its first report, on Hertfordshire, in 1910. This rhythm of work was not maintained, as we shall see later. The Commission was a body of scholars without powers, and already within four years of its foundation its Chairman was complaining that the public believed it had powers to protect historic monuments, instead of merely publishing them and assessing their importance.[1]

The Acts of 1882 and 1900 had made little difference to the situation. In the thirty years since the former had been passed, not a single ancient monument had been acquired for the state, though 104 had been taken into guardianship. Expenditure was running at £20,000 annually, of which £9,000 went to the Tower of London. Of that £9,000, £8,200 went on the wages of warders and policemen, and only £800 on the fabric. The portion of the total £20,000 which went on actual maintenance was £3,000.

But worse than this was the fact that ancient monuments were still wholly without protection against the only people likely to harm them, namely such of their owners as wished to do so. A case arose in 1911 which was dramatic enough to jolt public opinion, and thus the government, into action at last. High above the Lincolnshire flats there still just stood the great tower of Tattershall Castle, which had not gone the way of the stone buildings surrounding it because you cannot burn bricks for lime. The following account of what happened next is given by Lord Curzon.

The famous old red-brick castle of Tattershall in Lincoln-

---

[1] House of Lords debates on the 1912 bill; see p. 34.

shire, and the four sculptured stone mantelpieces which were made for it by its founder Lord Cromwell in 1440, and contain the armorial bearings of himself and his family alliances, and are unique in the world, were sold by the family to whom they had belonged for centuries in 1910. Subsequently, upon the purchaser of the estate becoming bankrupt, they passed into the hands of a Lincoln Bank, to whom the Estate had been mortgaged, and were sold by them in 1911. The Castle was presently acquired by an American Syndicate of speculators, who looked only to profit. The mantelpieces were sold separately from the Castle and were bought by a London firm of art dealers, and again disposed of by them to a German dealer, with partners in America, where it has all along been intended to offer them for sale.

The attention of the public having been called to the sale of the Castle and to the abstraction of the mantelpieces, which were carried off by the dealers to London, and an abortive attempt to save both having been made by the National Trust for Places of Historic Interest, I was led in the past autumn to look into the question by my interest in archaeological matters, and my strong feeling against the destruction or spoliation of one of the foremost and most splendid of our national monuments.

Finding that there was a very serious and imminent danger that the Castle might be pulled down, or otherwise ruined, by the American Syndicate, and learning that there was an interval of twenty-four hours in the course of which it could still be recovered by the payment of a certain profit to them, I intervened to rescue it. [1]

Perhaps this is the story that lies behind the film *The Ghost Goes West* made some twenty years later. If American dealers were ready to take the gigantic and magnificent fifteenth century stone fireplaces from an English castle, it was perhaps only the fact that it was built of brick that prevented them from taking the whole.

[1]Marquis Curzon and H. A. Tipping *Tattershall Castle*, Cape, 1929, p. 142.

It was at least in part this dramatic and well-publicised last minute rescue which finally drove Parliament to pass an Act in 1913 which contained the first halting and cumbrous provisions for compulsion. Just as the Conservative governments had resisted Lubbock's first attempt, and it had taken a Liberal government to permit the 1882 Act to reach the Statute Book, so now once again it was a member of a Liberal government, Lord Beauchamp, the First Commissioner of Works, who introduced into the House of Lords in 1912 the Ancient Monuments Consolidation Bill. This Bill provided that the Commissioners of Works could (when recommended to do so by an advisory board) make a Preservation Order in respect of a particular scheduled monument. The order would fall unless confirmed by a bill in Parliament which would have to resemble a private bill. This meant that any objector, normally the owner, would have the right to petition against it before a Committee of Parliament. The Ancient Monuments Consolidation Bill also gave the Commissioners the right of pre-emptive purchase; that is to say, first refusal when the owner sold, particularly, of course, in order to prevent export to America. On the other hand, the penalty was so slight as to deprive these provisions of effect; it was five pounds. Lord Burghclere, the Chairman of the Royal Commission on Historical Monuments, pointed out in debate that this might be enough to deter collectors from knocking bits off and carrying them away, but it would not be enough to stiffen an owner against the blandishments of American millions. (And indeed the penalty was raised in Parliament to £100.)

The Duke of Rutland chimed in with the familiar line: 'There is a great tendency nowadays to set up State interference with private property, and it is a moot point how far that can be carried without inflicting unnecessary and sometimes almost brutal hardship on the owner.' It was quite unjust to deprive him of his 'larger price in the open market'. One had only to look

at Italy where the law against the sale of works of art
had proved most onerous for the owner 'and the unfortunate people who live on the owner's estates', who might
have profited much from the sales.

It was at this point in the debate that Curzon intervened with a speech which did much to stiffen the
Government's resolve, and which went clean against the
traditional philistinism of his own party. He was then
in his period of eclipse. His years as the dynamic young
Viceroy who had reformed everything in India, and in
the end reformed himself out of a job, were behind
him. The haughty foreign secretary, to whom for the
next fifty years all stories of aristocratic pachydermy were
attached, was still to come. Curzon berated Lord Beauchamp for speaking for only seven minutes, 'because
this is a matter in which I have taken great interest. . . .
To those who take an interest in ancient monuments it
is a very important measure indeed, and I came down
to the House with the hope of hearing the noble Earl
discourse upon it for a period of least half an hour,
and I should have been content even to listen to him
for an hour. . . But he treated the Bill as if it were a
perfunctory matter. . . I do not feel thereby dispensed
from making a few observations on the subject.'

In recent years, the attitude of this country (and
others) had changed towards archaeology: monuments
were now regarded as part of the heritage and history
of the nation . . . documents just as valuable in reading
the records of the past as is any manuscript or parchment
deed. 'Owners now recognise that they are not merely
owners of private property, but trustees to the nation at
large.' English ancient monuments were of special
importance because they were also part of the heritage
and history of 'our kith and kin from America or the
Colonies', who have no monuments of their own. Curzon
was far-sighted enough to wish to include in the definition of ancient monuments not only stone circles and
castles, but also mansion houses, manor houses, 'and

then, descending the scale, the smaller buildings,
whether they be bridges, market crosses, cottages or even
barns, which carry on their face the precious story of
the past.' England was unusually rich in monuments
because of her 'less troubled history', but 'you only have
to study the records of this matter to see that the number
is diminishing from year to year and almost from day
to day.' Everywhere 'a certain amount of destruction is
brought about by the ravages of time, but even more has
been wrought by indifference, carelessness, vandalism
and the needless utilitarianism of the day.' The 1882 Act
was now recognised to have been so mild as to have been
useless, and 'if this Bill passes into law in its present
form, twenty years hence it will be looked upon as a
ridiculously mild and inoffensive Bill also'. The present
Bill was at last 'a recognition of responsibility, too long
delayed, which the State ought certainly to assume.' At
that time there was nothing but public opinion to prevent ancient monuments being sold to America, and
'public opinion is a very insecure guarantee in matters
of taste and antiquity and art'. As for rights of property:
'As long as a man treats the monument in his possession
well and reverently, this Bill makes no interference with
him at all.' The right of pre-emption was not really
necessary as Commissioners of Works already had (since
1882) power to purchase by agreement. 'I think I am
correct in saying that not one penny of public money
has been devoted to the purchase of existing monuments
. . . and the same would apply under this Bill.' The
Treasury never had found and never would find the
money. So why not forget about pre-emption, since it
alarmed needlessly?

Curzon ended by reminding the House that he had
himself introduced a Bill for protection of ancient monuments in India in 1904, despite objections about rights
of property. The Act had worked well in India, and that
was a good omen for this Bill. No doubt a good many
people present had seen Curzon's own restorations in

Delhi and Agra.

The debate thereafter abounded in expressions of imperial confidence. One peer alleged that when a few years back the owner of Stonehenge had threatened to sell it to America unless the Chancellor of the Exchequer bought it, the latter 'replied with a very proper spirit that if any such thing were attempted, the Government would send a military force to prevent it. . . I think that is the tone and temper in which this subject of ancient monuments and their possible removal across the Atlantic ought to be approached.' Lord Crewe, the Leader of the House, gave it as his opinion that ancient monuments were more neglected in England than, for example, in Italy, because of the revenue that the latter derived from tourism, so that the loss of Italian monuments would be a national disaster. In England, we were not affected by tourists, 'and as a country I do not know that we very much care, from the point of view of our pockets, whether they come or not.' The Bill, and two others which had been introduced into the House of Lords at the same time, were committed to a Joint Select Committee of both Houses of Parliament.

The Committee hearings were notable for the evidence of Charles Reed Peers, Inspector of Ancient Monuments under the 1882 Act, and Secretary of the Society of Antiquaries. Time was to confirm the need for many of the things he put his finger on then. The 1882 Act, he said, was so excessively mild that most people, including many owners, had never heard of it. The most important part of the new bill was the preservation orders, and it was vital not to emasculate them. But the Bill had defects. Above all, it was too narrowly drawn in that it still did not apply to buildings in use. He would like to see it extended in that way, and to see the State enabled to contribute to the upkeep of inhabited monuments, and thus to acquire a voice in what was done to them. An advisory Board could tell it how to use this voice in respect of each particular building. These things were done, exactly as Peers and Curzon wished, in 1932, 1947 and 1953.

Another interesting statement was made to the Committee by Edward Owen, Secretary of the Royal Commission on Historical Monuments in Wales. When he went inspecting his ancient monuments the people most helpful to him were postmen, policemen, and schoolteachers, and the best places to learn and talk about the monuments were the smithy and the tailor's shop. It has long been known to those who know any-thing about all this that the statement that working class people are not interested in preservation is very seldom made by working class people. Indeed in reading this evidence before the 1912 Committee one is struck by how little it all changes. An aluminium smelter in Scotland; a cinema advertisement ruining Hexham; gas-holders towering over little towns. But, cries the Chair-man: 'Where are you going to stop in a matter which is really one of aesthetics? . . . Care must be taken not to overload the bill and turn public opinion against it.'

When the Bill came out of Committee, it ran once again into the already familiar criticism of its limitations in the House of Commons. Mr King, member for North Somerset, said:

I consider that a dwelling house may be an extremely important ancient monument, and that it should be pro-tected. What is more interesting and instructive than to see the sort of house in which our ancestors lived? . . . I want the Committee to realise that, some day or other, either we or those who come after us will be wise enough to protect the ancient monuments which remain in dwelling houses.

But this change was not made then. The Bill duly became the Ancient Monuments Act of 1913, and the British Government had its first preservation powers.

The decades between the two World Wars saw some sensible advances. An Act of 1931 provided that preser-vation orders on ancient monuments need not each be separately confirmed by an act of Parliament unless there was an objection to them, and an Act of 1933 provided that, even if there was an objection, this could be heard at a public enquiry and need no longer be heard before a select committee of Parliament.

But the most important law was the Town and Country Planning Act of 1932. This Act was introduced by Sir Hilton Young, then Minister of Health and Housing, who later became the first Lord Kennet, and was the present writer's father. It got rid for the first time of the restrictive principle that, to be a proper subject of preservation by the State, a building of historic interest must be uninhabited or inhabited only by a caretaker. It allowed local authorities to make, vary or revoke a 'preservation order' in respect of any building in their area which was of 'special architectural or historic interest'. Each such order had to be individually approved by the Minister, and the latter was bound to 'consider any representation made to him by the owner of the building or by any other person' and to 'consult with the Commissioners of Works' (who administered the Ancient Monuments law). Once the Order was in force by the Minister's approval, the owner could still apply to the local council to vary or revoke it, and if he refused could appeal to the Minister. The Act did not apply to ecclesiastical buildings in use as such, or to buildings already covered by the antecedent Ancient Monuments legislation. There was a provision for compensation to any person whose 'legal rights in respect of' the relevant property were 'infringed or curtailed' by the Preservation Order. Preservation Orders could also be placed on trees, groups of trees, and areas of woodland. An order to demolish advertisement hoardings injuring amenity could be given and, if the owner refused, the hoardings could be forcibly removed by the local authority, which could then recover its expenses from the owner.

In introducing the Bill, Sir Hilton Young made the hopeful claim that it was 'to a very large extent uncontroversial' and 'wholly non-partisan'. The preservation part of the Bill (the rest was about what we would now call planning in general, and had a slum clearance slant to it) had its origins in his own attempt three or four years before to pass a Private Member's Bill on the protection of the amenities of the countryside. All the local authority associations had been asking for legislation of this sort and no fewer than eighteen private acts already existed giving particular local authorities the powers which would be made general by the Bill. In an age of rising population and urban expansion, it was necessary to protect the countryside so that there was something for town dwellers to see when they got there.

For the Labour Party, Sir Stafford Cripps endorsed the Bill: 'The general principle of the measure is in accord with what we believe to be the best social practice.'

The mainline Tory attack (for the bill was not a typical Tory measure) came from Sir Derek Walker-Smith: 'This is just the kind of measure that a Socialist government would introduce. An enormous amount of power and control over rights of property are invested in local authority and government departments.' Lord Hartington said it was all wrong to give the power to the local authorities who were 'the greatest offenders and have been guilty of wholesale vandalism'. It was the voluntary bodies such as the Council for the Preservation of Rural England which could and should persuade the local authorities to use the immense powers they already had. Mr Buchan said Lord Hartington had delighted the House with 'that fine, stalwart, massive thing, the true Whig creed' and rejoiced that 'one famous historic monument, the Whig point of view' would never decay as long as the Noble Marquis lived. The Bill got through and its preservation provisions passed into law largely in their original form. About twenty Preservation Orders were made under it before the system was reformed by the 1947 Act: six of these were in the little borough of New Romney, where the mayor was an antiquary.

The decades between the wars also saw a considerable

development in voluntary activity, and a beginning of state concessions to favour voluntary activity.

In the twenties and thirties the estate duty, or death duty, which had been greatly increased by Lloyd George in his famous budget of 1910, began to bite on the great families, and England was faced with the probable disappearance, over a couple of generations, of those very country houses which according to a widely accepted judgement were her greatest contribution to the visual arts. The National Trust decided to change the emphasis of its work in order to avert this threat. In the mid-thirties, acting largely under the impulsion of the then Lord Lothian, who had inherited Blickling in 1930 and had had to sell much of its great library to America in order to pay the estate duty on it, the National Trust approached successive Chancellors of the Exchequer to seek a scheme by which owners of fine houses should be exempted from estate duty. Since 1910, people had been allowed to leave works of art to the State instead of their heirs having to sell them to someone else in order to raise money to give to the State. The National Trust conceived that fine houses should be treated the same way.

And so they were, but only slowly and by degrees. The 1910 Finance Act (the same Lloyd George budget which stepped up the Estate Duty, and led to the constitutional crisis of 1910-11) had given the Inland Revenue power to accept land and buildings instead of cash in payment of death duties. But the First World War was not far off, and in all the Conservative years of the peace between the two wars this power was used only twice, once to transfer a trivial property to the Post Office, and once to a local authority.

In 1927 the Finance Act gave the National Trust certain help in setting up its country house scheme. But still nothing was done which would have the effect of bringing the 1910 powers into use on a scale sufficient to preserve the greatest houses of the heritage. It was not until the arrival of a Labour government after the victory of 1945 that the National Trust's twenty-year-old vision was brought to reality. In his budget speech for 1946, Hugh Dalton as Chancellor of the Exchequer announced the creation as a 'thank offering for victory' of a National Land Fund of £50 million the money to be derived from the sale of surplus war stores and to be used for acquiring and preserving property in the national interest. This money was to make possible the systematic use of Lloyd George's power of 1910. Speaking of the National Trust and other such non-profit making bodies Dalton said: 'We regard them as friends of the public interest, and we desire to help them.'

Many variants have developed under this system, but broadly what happens is that when the owner of a house the National Trust considers up to its standard dies, the heir can make over the house to the State in lieu of duty. The State then gives the house to the National Trust, and the Trust allows the heir to go on living there as its tenant, usually in one corner, while the rest (though often that corner too) is thrown open to the public. The only drawback to the scheme, which is now a very real one, is that it does not give the Trust any money to keep the house up. The Trust will not now accept houses unless the family can make an upkeep endowment with the gift, or unless the State can guarantee maintenance grants with the transfer; and this the State increasingly does.

The history is a very English one. A sweeping egalitarian tax is found in time to have a socially undesirable side effect; a voluntary body thinks up a monstrously complicated scheme to get round it, and is graciously permitted by the State to put it into effect. Finally the State starts paying grants to the voluntary body to help it run the scheme.

It was also in 1937, the year of the important National Trust Act, that the Georgian Group was set up, thus breaking from the SPAB. Though it is hard to believe this now, when the Group has been so successful, the reason for the split was that Georgian buildings were not really regarded in those days as worthy of preservation, and those who cared especially for them found that a new and specialised society was needed. To read of the early days of the Georgian Group is to wonder at the progress there has been in the last generation. In those days, Nancy Mitford threatened to tie herself naked to the railings of the Houses of Parliament. This is rough: this is unlike the world we know. But so were the threats to be averted. Brighton Corporation was in the middle of one of its regular attempts to pull down the Pavilion, and the London highway authorities were trying to pull down the whole West side of Bedford Square in order to widen Tottenham Court Road. We should count our blessings.

In 1940 the last all-out war between European nation states, taking the form of aerial bombardment, began to destroy the English heritage of architecture much more rapidly than anything had ever done before. The German bombs did not know whether a given building was uninhabited or inhabited only by a caretaker, in which case it was likely to have been scheduled as an ancient monument, and thus recorded, or was on the other hand inhabited by a family or by people working, in which case it was not. The Royal Commission set up thirty years before to record all historic buildings worthy of note regardless of the manner of their habitation had by then reported on eight of the forty-odd English counties. It was clear that since much would be lost, it would be advisable to know what. In the Town and Country Planning Act of 1944, Parliament therefore empowered the Minister of Town and Country Planning (whom it was then inventing) to prepare lists of buildings of special historic and architectural interest. These lists would no doubt be useful for planning the country after the war. They were intended partly as a record of what might be restored after bombing, or might still be bombed, and partly as a guide for local authorities in assuming their new planning functions.

The 1944 Act was succeeded by that of 1947 which is the foundation of our present land use planning system, by general consent the most advanced in the world. The 1944 Act provided for the definitive listing by central government of buildings whether or not they were inhabited: the 1947 Act consolidated and improved the local authorities power, given in 1932, to preserve them whether or not the owners wished them preserved. The same principles of central government intervention which had been introduced in 1913 to preserve the uninhabited ancient monuments were, in effect, now extended to the vastly wider field of inhabited buildings. (The 1932 Act had allowed only local government intervention.) The 1947 preservation provisions were part of a very long and very controversial bill. They were never discussed at all in the House of Commons, which was fully occupied with the first introduction into the law of any democratic country of the principle that society might forbid a man to do what he would with his own land, without compensation. That principle is the foundation of our whole system of land use planning and of any practical system of land use planning. It is also the foundation of our system of preservation law, and of any practical system of preservation law.

The 1947 debate in the House of Lords was on the whole not up to the standard of the earlier ones, for the same reason that there was no debate at all in the House of Commons. Another Marquess of Salisbury, but once again Leader of the Opposition, said: 'It is at least doubtful whether the local planning authorities are the right people to perform this particular function. . . The preservation of buildings of architectural and historic interest needs special knowledge. . . The danger is not that they will include too much, but that they will include too little.' He therefore favoured a more powerful role for the Minister of Works. Lord Harlech, a former First Commissioner of Works, related how he had been unable to prevent the Burgh Council of Dundee pulling down its Adam town hall, and drew from this the defensible moral that central power was to be preferred to local. Lord Chancellor Jowett for the government on the other hand said: 'I am very anxious in these days to maintain and support local pride.' Local authorities would resent any presumed loss of power and would thus do even less than they did to preserve historic buildings. Much of the debate was conducted in the mistaken belief that the bill would give local authorities power to take over neglected listed buildings, and sufficient funds to maintain them when they did.

After the war, the loss of great country houses continued in spite of Hugh Dalton's imaginative Land Fund, and a committee under Sir Ernest Gowers was set up to enquire into it. The Gowers Report appeared in 1950, and its most important recommendations were as follows:

  (i) That a statutory body (to be called the Historic Buildings Council) should be created for England and Wales, and another for Scotland, and entrusted with duties both general and specific for furthering the preservation of houses of outstanding historic or architectural interest . . .

(xiv) That the owner-occupiers of designated houses should be entitled to the following tax reliefs subject to showing their houses to the public . . .

    (a) Relief from income tax and surtax in respect of approved expenditure on repairs to and maintenance of the house and contents . . .

    (b) Relief from death duties on the house, listed contents and amenity land so long as they are not sold . . .

    (c) Relief from death duties . . . on property assigned to trustees to maintain the house out of the income of the property . . .

(xviii)That the Historic Buildings Councils should have
wide powers of aiding the preservation of designated
houses and their listed contents (including houses
owned by local authorities or the National Trusts) by
giving expert advice; by themselves carrying out works
of repair and maintenance; and by loans and grants
at their discretion on such terms and conditions as
they think fit.

(xix) That the (Historic Buildings) Councils should have
power to acquire designated houses, their contents and
the amenity land by agreement, or compulsorily if that
is necessary to preserve them, and to hold and manage
properties so acquired until some suitable use can be
found by which they can be preserved.

In 1953 a bill was therefore introduced into Parliament allowing the Minister of Works to make grants for
the restoration and maintenance of historic buildings and
their contents, and setting up a Historic Buildings Council to advise him how to do it, but not taking up the
Gowers Report's proposals on tax relief and on compulsory power to purchase. In introducing the Bill, the
Minister of Works, Sir David Eccles, said that the kinds
of houses for which it was intended to make grants were
the best examples of all styles, whether big or small,
in town or country. The Historic Buildings Councils
(English, Scottish and Welsh) could not indeed be
expected to be 'entirely immune from prevailing
fashion', but they would do their best. As an example
of the way fashion changes he gave the building in
which he was speaking, Barry's Palace of Westminster,
which was in turn admired, then 'disapproved of—I
choose a very moderate word', and now appeared to be
regaining its popularity. Buildings with historical associations would also be favoured: whether these associations were with events, owners or a matter of long
connection with one family. And lastly he would rather
spend enough on a limited number of buildings than
spread the butter too thin over larger numbers.

Hugh Dalton from the Opposition bench asked, as well he might, what had happened to the Land Fund that he introduced. He had meant it to be spent; instead of which the original £50 million he set up now stood at £54 million. Why did the Government not spend that money now, on grants and purchases? No answer forthcame.

Mr Kenneth Robinson, on behalf of the National Trust, said that the Bill ought to have enabled the Minister to provide endowments for the Trust, and, even more important, to supplement inadequate endowments made by donors.

There is a limit to the interest which a reader will feel in debates so recent as this and in the words of politicians who are still with us. But I cannot forbear from resurrecting Mr Jo Grimond's words:

'I do not particularly mind about the owner's position, but it makes a lot of ordinary people very happy to get into a bus or a charabanc and to go off to see beautiful houses . . . What the visitors enjoy is not only seeing beautiful pictures or architecture. They enjoy seeing the blotting paper bearing the imprint of the owner's last letter, and that sort of thing . . . It gives pleasure to people who go out for their Saturday afternoons and Sundays to find the owners of these houses at home.'

When the Bill came before the House of Lords, Lord Silkin, the architect of the great 1947 Planning Act, agreed that preservation was important, but what for? Beautiful historic houses should be lived in, and not become museums. But how many people were going to be able to afford to live in the two thousand houses which were worthy of preservation? The problem was not only money, but also servants; and possible uses for those houses were limited, unless their character were to be destroyed. 'It is an awful thing to say about these houses that they should be allowed to go to ruin, but I am pointing out some of the difficulties . . . which Sir

Ernest Gowers and his committee have not faced up to completely.' Moreover, would heavily taxed people consent to tax relief or subsidy for people 'very much better off than themselves to enable them to live in these large mansions?' It would cost ten million a year to implement the report.

Lord Silkin was gently put in his place by Lord Lawson, one of the few peers who had ever been an industrial worker. If these beautiful places, he said, which could be made useful as hospitals, schools and so on, are not saved, 'nobody in this country would be more sorry than the average industrial worker who in some cases has had to spend his life within sight of these places but is not always very familiar with them.'

The Bill passed into law, and the Historic Buildings Councils were set up. In each of its first four years, the Minister of Housing spent on the advice of the English Council successively £298,000, £142,000, £243,000 and £333,000. When in 1958 it spent £548,000 the Treasury decided enough was enough, and imposed a ceiling of £400,000 a year.

The Town and Country Planning Act of 1962, which consolidated and improved much of the general system of planning in the country, continued the 1947 provisions about historic buildings. In 1962 also, Parliament passed a private member's bill, introduced by Mr Paul Channon, which empowered local authorities to make their own grants out of the rates for the upkeep and maintenance of any building, not necessarily listed, which they considered of architectural or historic interest. Buckinghamshire County Council uses it and so does Chester City. Elsewhere it has remained virtually a dead letter.

II

Recent changes

From 1966 to 1970 the present writer was personally connected with the development of legislation, policy and finance on the preservation of buildings of historic or architectural interest. So the ensuing narrative of what happened is bound to be a bit egocentric. But egocentricity does not always make for boredom, so here goes.

When Harold Wilson was constructing his government after the 1966 election, he sent for me, and I hoped it would be a Foreign Office appointment since that was the direction in which my political life had lain so far. He said: Ministry of Housing and Local Government, parliamentary secretary. I protested my lack of knowledge and experience, and he countered with two points. First, that Prime Ministers always started junior ministers off in what they considered the wrong place; it had happened to him when Attlee made him parliamentary secretary at the Ministry of Works in 1945 instead of something on the welfare state side, which he considered he was qualified for. And second, I would be able to look after historic buildings. The latter point was well judged, since, ten years before, my wife and I had written a book about Old London Churches, and I had retained an interest in the history of architecture, and in urban design. It was this remark, together with a sense that however little I knew about them, housing, planning and local government in general were important, that decided me to accept rather than to continue talking about foreign affairs in the press and from

49

the back benches.

The Minister of Housing and Local Government was then Richard Crossman, and he was assisted by five sub-ordinate ministers; Fred Willey, whose ill-starred Ministry of Land and Natural Resources was being reabsorbed into the parent Ministry of Housing and Local Government for reasons well outside the scope of this book, Robert Mellish, Arthur Skeffington, James MacColl, and me.

Mr Crossman had recently held a weekend study con-ference on the preservation of historic towns, at Churchill College, Cambridge, which had revealed to him how little was known about the whole problem. He had also taken the first measure to stop the running down of the administrative staff who looked after preser-vation under the 1947 Act; this had been going on for some years. When the Conservative Government came in in 1951, they had reduced the establishment of Inves-tigators, as the experts are called who make the 'list',[1] from twenty-four to twelve and later to nine. He was also in the process of securing the transfer from the Minister of Works to himself of the power to pay grants for restoration (and sometimes upkeep) to the owners of buildings listed as being of architectural or historic importance. These were the grants paid on the advice of the Historic Buildings Council which was set up as we have seen by the Historic Monuments Act of 1953, after the Gowers Report. In 1953 it had no doubt seemed a good idea that this administration should go with that of the Ancient Monuments themselves, because of the Inspectors of Ancient Monuments and the corps of antiquarian architects at the Ministry of Works. But over the years it had become clear that it would be better placed with the administration of the planning system in general. This rested with the Minister of Housing and Local Government, and with the control of the

[1]See p. 53.

building preservation order system which had been transferred to him in 1962. Only thus would the minister who ran the system which decided whether historic buildings should be pulled down be able to frame his policies in the light of the knowledge whether or not the owners of such buildings might hope for grants to help keep them standing up. Even so, the function was by no means transferred without bloodshed in Whitehall, and it was several weeks after the Election before it was clear that Crossman was going to win. I was too new to join in the battle, and watched it with awestruck incredulity. So much so that I later on readily accepted the official advice against finishing the job by bringing over the ancient monuments as well; the advice was that more bloodshed would, for some years, be a bad thing. Luckily all this was overtaken by the larger amalgamation which gave rise to the Department of the Environment after the Conservatives won the election of 1970, an amalgamation which would also have taken place if Labour had won.

I reported the Prime Minister's remark to Crossman, and said I thought that was a good idea. In fact, I asked for the historic buildings job, among the many functions which fell to a Minister of Housing and Local Government. Crossman let me have it, and this was pleasant of him since he had been doing it himself without assistance from a junior minister and had, I think, been enjoying it pretty well. It is enjoyable; not many beautiful things come into a minister's life.

For some years now the English had been steadily and rapidly emerging from an age of blindness. How that blindness started, how it overcame the descendants of Hawksmoor and Blake and Butterfield, is a mystery that awaits elucidation by someone with a deeper knowledge of the interaction of art and society than I have. But sure it is that the second quarter of the twentieth century was our low-water mark in visual consciousness. Our buildings were dull, we dressed abominably, the things we used were not so much ill designed as undesigned. Delight in beauty and care to learn its principles had already dried up before the rigours of war stopped building and made style in anything an unpatriotic expense.

After the Second World War, our eyes were opened again both by increasing wealth which led to foreign travel and, much more than that, by television. Millions of people who when they had nothing to do would formerly have opened a book, or turned on the radio, began instead to turn on the television which, true enough, usually uses only one eye; but half a pair is better than no look. In the fifties young people began to care once again how they dressed, and the standards of design, both in architecture and in general, shot up. The stately home business boomed, and is still booming. The owners of those great houses which were opened most successfully began to count their annual gate in hundreds of thousands. Sir Nikolaus Pevsner's great Penguin series *The Buildings of England* told all of us cheaply, rapidly and copiously, what good buildings there were to see, and gave us for background not thatch and hollyhocks but the whole history of European architecture. Sir John Betjeman re-awakened our visual nostalgia, but as an informed, not sentimental, nostalgia, and gave us enjoyment by sharing his own. There was a general shift of our national consciousness towards the visual, and a greater flow than ever of good and readable scholarship about architecture and the arts. Everywhere local amenity societies sprang to life, and more and more people became conscious that their street, their village, their town, their quarter of a city, was different from others because it had grown differently, and that that was interesting.

It was my job to see that, in the restricted field of the architectural heritage, no less than in others, the structure of public law and administration was adequate to meet this new and rightful public demand. The first step was to form my own impression of what, if anything, needed doing. The qualifying clause was quickly disposed of; in spite of, and sometimes because of, fifty years of state regulation, plenty did.

The foundation of the whole system of administration and statutory control was 'the list'. This was the list, compiled under the powers of the 1944 Act, of, at that time, about 90,000 buildings, which the minister's[1] advisers told him were of historical or architectural interest. It was the present day equivalent of Lubbock's first list of twenty-nine national monuments; these, and only these, were the concern of the law. The owner of a statutorily listed building was not allowed to destroy it until he had told the local authority of his intention, and had waited for two months to see if they objected. There was also the so-called 'supplementary list', where the minister just asked the local authority to consider whether the buildings might not be worth preserving, but nobody was bound to do anything about it by law. It contained about 100,000 buildings.

I naturally first asked at what rate the listed buildings were being destroyed, to get an idea of where we stood. I was prepared for the shock of a high figure; a hundred a year? Even two hundred a year? I was not prepared, though, for the answer I got: 'We don't know; and this is because nobody tells us; and this is because we have never asked anybody to tell us.' I marvelled at the willingness of Parliament to set up, and the Civil Service to operate, a system designed to have a certain effect without ever checking whether it was having that effect, or another, or none. I asked the officials to let me have a guess, even a wild one from whatever evidence they could rake together, of the rate of loss of listed buildings. I also went round the country a bit, and tried to form a

[1]In 1970 the powers of the Ministers of Housing and of Works, including their respective preservation powers, passed to the new Secretary of State for the Environment. In what follows 'the Minister' before 1970 and 'the Secretary of State' after 1970 are the same legal person.

subjective impression of how the historic buildings and towns were lasting out, and what kind of thing was put up in their place when they did not last out. I found a wide variety of situations, from the wanton and pointless destruction of the historic quarters of Poole and Gosport to the care and intelligence, limited only by lack of funds, which were to be seen at Winchester and Bath; from the hideous and ridiculous intrusions of the Norwich Union Building in Peterborough, and Stonebow House at York, to the wonderful cunning and grace of the Cripps Building at St John's College, Cambridge. This last, though, had been very expensive.

Next it seemed a good idea to have a look at what was being done in other countries. Of our European neighbours with comparable population and a comparable architectural heritage, Germany was clearly less relevant because of its federal constitution, and Russia, Poland, Czechoslovakia, and Spain were so because of their lack of democratic institutions. I chose France and Italy, and visited both during the summer of 1966. This was four years after the Malraux Law on urban preservation and restoration had come into effect in France.

Until 1962, French preservation law had been based solely on the lists of *monuments* and *sites*: *monuments* are usually single buildings, and *sites* are hilltop villages, ruined castles, etc. They might or might not be state property. The *monuments* were (and still are) divided into two categories: *monuments classés*, which may not be demolished or altered without the permission of the central government, and *monuments inscrits* which may not be demolished or altered without allowing the central government time to object. Until 1966, the state had been liable to compensate the owner of a building, on *classement*, for the loss of development value, but at the time of my visit they were reducing the entitlement to compensation so that it covered only the loss of improvement in the present use. (For instance, a town householder would no longer be compensated for not being allowed to pull down his house and put up an office block, only for not being allowed to pull it down and put up a more modern house.)

I asked what happened if someone broke the law and demolished a *monument classé* or *inscrit* without going through its procedures. I gathered that it had never happened, but the owner of a town house which was a *monument classé* had once asked what he would be allowed to build on the site if he illegally demolished it; he had been told 'a lawn'.

But the greatest difference between French law and English is the *zone protégé*. This is a circle no less than one kilometre in diameter surrounding every single *monument* and *site classé* in the land, in which all demolition and new building has to be approved by the central government. Since there are no historic towns and few historic villages without a church or chateau in the middle which is a *monument classé*, this gives the state negative planning control of virtually the entire French architectural heritage. No such provision existed in England.

It seemed to me that the pre-Malraux law of preservation in France was inferior to ours in making it the duty of the state to pay compensation on *classement*, and in the consequently lower number of buildings protected; 26,000 against about 100,000. (Now 29,000 against 119,000 respectively.) It seemed superior to ours in the protection it gave against ugly or over-large new development provided by the *zones protégés*.

The Malraux law of 1962 transformed the situation in that it installed for the first time not indeed the protection of groups or areas—that was there already in the *zones protégés*—but the active intervention of public bodies to restore groups or areas, called for this purpose *secteurs sauvegardés*. I visited three *secteurs sauvegardés*: the Marais in Paris, the Quartier St Jean in Lyon, and the Quartier de la Balance in Avignon.

The buildings in each of these are quite different. The

Marais is a whole quarter of the old city of Paris; 125
hectares (c. 309 acres). There is an 'Operational Sector'
of 8½ hectares (c. 21 acres), and within that an 'Attack
Sector' of 3 hectares (c. 7 acres). The Marais contains
several dozen *hôtels particuliers* of the sixteenth, seventeenth and eighteenth centuries, probably all of which
would be Grade I in England. Between and among these
there is a mass of good solid seventeenth and eighteenth
century housing. The density of houses of the highest
architectural interest is hard to parallel in any English
city except Oxford, Cambridge and Bath. Often the
courtyards of the *hôtels* are glazed over, and extra blocks
conceal various swoops and loggias of the Renaissance,
of Mannerism, of the Age of Reason. As he goes there
more frequently to the open-air plays and concerts which
are being laid on to attract him, the ordinary tourist will
probably be amazed, as I was, at the wealth of wonderful
buildings standing neglected half a mile from the beaten
track.

The Quartier St Jean in Lyon is smaller; it is a
solid mass of tall town housing of the fifteenth, sixteenth
and seventeenth centuries, left by a flourishing culture
of Italian bankers and merchants from the Renaissance.
You go in from canyon streets through a vaulted passage-
way called a *traboule* (*tra-buco*, hole through?) into one
or a series of deep inner courtyards. There are nearly
a thousand of these courtyards. One is by Serlio himself,
one by Philibert de l'Orme; hundreds have good, or
funny, appliqué features. It is a sort of postage stamp
history of French architecture.

The Quartier de la Balance in Avignon is basically
a sixteenth and seventeenth century quarter without any
architecture, but providing a visual podium for the
Palace of the Popes, which is one of the greatest com-
plexes of medieval churches and palaces in Europe. The
Balance has to be kept because anything else under those
white walls and towers would look awful.

The people in the three places were also different. In

the Marais the *hôtels* were typically full of artisan industry: makers of toys, dolls, bowler hats, musical instruments, and bookbinders. The other houses were full of artisans and shop-keepers. There were small free-holders, and many tenants and sub-tenants; often fifty occupants in a *hôtel*. The quarter was run-down, but not slummy.

In Lyon also, it was dwellings, and small shops. The ownership pattern was about the same as in the Marais; 26% owner occupiers, 74% tenants. All was poor, and parts were the vilest slum I had ever seen in Europe, Naples not excluded.

In Avignon, there were three special groups. Gypsies had settled there as squatters after the rent controls of 1914-18. There were *harkis*, Muslim supernumaries who had fought with the French army in the Algerian war and at the end of it had had to be 'repatriated' to France with their families to save their lives. Thirdly, there were prostitutes. Many bourgeois of Avignon die without ever having set foot in this famous red-light quarter. The housing ranged from poor to infra-slum, meaning squatters with no roof, just walls. There were a few small shops. In all three places, the people were poorer than in the historic centres of English cities.

There was little traffic in any of the three areas. A declared aim is pedestrianisation of the sectors and this should not be too difficult as through-traffic already passes the areas by, generally adhering to the obvious main roads. The small streets would not be able to absorb more traffic, and if the population of the sectors becomes wealthier, the ownership of cars will certainly rise greatly and present a problem. The French officials had foreseen this and in Lyon proposed to provide multi-storey garages outside the sector, a five minute walk away.

That was how things stood, and if nothing had been done those fine quarters would have been lost. So the plans were set afoot as follows. First, social and architec-

tural surveys of the sectors were made by teams under
an architectural consultant chosen by the government.
He was paid entirely by the Government; one third
came from the Ministry of Culture (which was in general
control of the application of the 1962 Law), and two
thirds from the Ministry of Equipment, which was
charged with the housing drive in general, and directly
in charge of environmental construction (roads, services,
etc.). That was the normal pattern, but in Avignon the
preliminary studies were financed by the general
development company (see below) and the actual designs
for restoration and new building by the companies which
were doing that work.

Physically, the plans consisted of a mixture of demolition and new construction, of alteration, of restoration,
and of leaving be. Street and pavement widths, and
parking arrangements, were taken out of the hands of
the ordinary departments and given to the preservation
planners. But there was still friction with the highway
authority on traffic control, and with other departments
on unsuitable buidings; usually schools. In the Marais, it
was clearly going to be a long time before they got
beyond the *curettage* and *lavage* (scraping off of excre-
scences, and washing) as a result of which they hoped a
new prosperity will be conceived in these magnificent
hôtels. They were also planning to re-create the open
places shown on a map of 1739. They spoke of a hundred-
year, or at best a fifty-year programme.

In Lyon they were beginning by taking later additions
off the tops of old houses, and running together two or
more old courts into one, to bring light and air to rooms
which are intolerable by modern standards.

In Avignon they had demolished a whole block. In
order to fit the new roofline in among the old ones, they
had adopted a pleasant plan. M le Vice-Directeur set up
a number of lighter-than-air balloons on strings marked
off for length, and numbered each balloon. M le Direc-
teur retreated to the top of another castle a mile or two

away with field-glasses and a walkie-talkie, and gave
instructions. 'Number three up a little; up a little more.
Number eighteen down. . . .' Then they read off the
heights, and released the balloons to the great joy of all
the children. Unfortunately the new block built there is
all the same lumpish and has proved unpopular. Some
streets, on the other hand, were being virtually rebuilt
behind existing façades. The first sample flats were
visible, and there was a waiting list of 350-400 intending
purchasers. The work had been done with skill and
imagination, producing a neat, clean and ancient look,
like a very good opera set for Monteverdi.

It was obvious that the difficulty inherent in this
heroic approach was going to be the rehousing of the
people displaced. In the Marais rehousing had hardly
begun. In Lyon they had some experience already. The
following alternative systems were offered to freeholders.

1 Carry out the approved plan yourself
2 Appoint Company as your agent, and pay the whole
3 The Company buys the freehold at an agreed price
4 The Company expropriates you under the 'public
   interest' provisions in the Law, at valuation, with
   appeal on valuation to the Courts

At that time only about thirty families had moved. None
chose system 1, fifteen chose system 2, eleven chose system
3, four were 'recalcitrant' and landed up with system 4.
When they move, the families take potluck on the municipal housing list, without priority. There is a system of
points for priority in rehousing in France, but I was not
able to find out what had happened to the departing
freeholders, let alone to their tenants.

In Avignon they had shifted 700 households from 140
houses (two or three thousand persons). Three hundred
households had been rehoused in two new special
developments side by side on the outskirts; one for
gypsies, one for *harkis*. There was a common community

centre, but feeling was already running high between the two groups; the *harki* housing was better. It gets a subsidy from the Minister of the Interior. (This problem was not, of course, intrinsic to the preservation of old towns.) All these 700 households were shifted under system 3. In Avignon, they claimed they had been able to avoid any expropriation because they had had explanatory discussions with the residents before they started, which had been fuller than those at Lyon. There, they admitted, these discussions had been inadequate. In both cities there was a feeling that rehousing arrangements are so far insufficient, and that 'we are only shifting the difficulties from one quarter to another.'

There was general agreement in all three places that there must be four new uses:

1 Middle-high income housing
2 Prestige shops with historically correct fascias (*bibelots*, pictures, maps, binderies, music)
3 Local shops and artisanate (grocers and re-bottomers of chairs) and
4 City-wide cultural and recreational uses

Museums are everywhere among the first incomers. Dance clubs. Yoga. Learned societies. String quartets. Jazz. Avignon was the best advanced: there new tenants were queueing. In Paris and Lyon, though the museums were willing, ordinary life had not yet committed itself. It hardly could have yet; there was nothing to see. Nowhere was there any sign of the original people being able to afford to come back, though the plans provide that they should if they can. In Paris one millionaire owner had restored his *hôtel* under the guidance of the scheme's architects; this was a show-piece which would attract other millionaires, but hardly doctors and engineers.

The finance and organisation were thus. When the initial studies, paid for by the Government, are approved, a development company takes over. The planning consultant (still paid by the Government) stays on to study later 'attack areas' while development begins on the first. The funds used for development are the ordinary funds for urban renewal, plus an extra government subsidy from the Ministry of Equipment (NB: not Culture) to cover the higher cost per room. Ordinary development is subsidised at a lower rate. The cost is higher for restoration because the buildings are lower than new development, thus land costs are higher, and because special materials and skills are needed. The cost per room, leaving out land value, was normally lower for restoration on these schemes than for new building. The cost of the initial studies is not included in these calculations.

Urban renewal in France, that is, urban renewal in any context, whether historic or not, is carried out by quite a different capital structure from the English one. The normal instrument is the 'mixed-economy company', meaning 51% owned by the municipality concerned, and 49% by private finance. I had the impression a fuller enquiry would reveal that a large amount of the whole is government money going round in circles. The mixed-economy companies themselves are often subsidiaries of the Caisse des Depots, which is a public body, something perhaps half-way between the Public Trustee and the Public Works Loan Board, but having very large resources at its disposal, including pension funds which in England are in the hands of the large insurance companies. A separate development company sometimes exists solely for the *secteur sauvegardé* operation: the one at Lyon is called Semirely; Société d'Economie Mixte pour la Restauration du Vieux Lyon, and the Mayor is Chairman of the company. At Avignon on the other hand the preservation work is carried out by a mixed company (Société d'Equipement du Département de Vaucluse) which operates in the whole Department of Vaucluse. But the Mayor of Avignon is Chairman just the same.

These development companies are entitled to raise
cheap loans (from the Crédit Foncier) for restoration
work, just as others are for normal development work.

I had expected, in accordance with stereotyped English
views about France, to find that everything was under
ruthless central control, and that powerless local councils were being swept along they knew not where. I
found on the contrary that not only was every effort
made to carry local government, but that sometimes local
government was spurring the centre. It is government
policy that the Mayor of whatever town is concerned
should not only guide and lead the operation, but should
actually be the chairman of the development company
doing the work. I got the impression that the towns
where it was most advanced were not those which the
government had decided to concentrate on, but those
where there was a strong mayor. In some cases I was
informed that the mayor, backed by a local preservation
society, had been agitating for precisely this arrangement
for some time before 1962, and had thus strengthened
M Malraux's hand in getting it through. In all three
cities, all the local political parties were backing the
operation, and in all three the more rigorous complexi-
ties of statute law were sensibly by-passed in the practice.
Il faut tourner la loi.

I next visited the Italian towns of Siena, Perugia and
Gubbio to see what was being done in that country about
the preservation of historic centres. These were the towns
chosen for me by the Fine Arts Department of the
Ministry of Education, which is the relevant Government Department.

Historic buildings in private ownership in Italy are
protected by a system which closely resembles the French.
The main difference is that in France there are 11,000
buildings which may not be demolished or altered without permission, and 15,000 which may not be demolished
or altered without notice, whereas in Italy there are
about 100,000 which may not be demolished or altered

without permission, and the fine for doing so may equal the development value of the site. The protection and restoration of historic centres is being tackled by a series of special laws—one each for Siena, Assisi, Genoa, Palermo, etc., which give the communes power of expropriation on the French model. An earlier attempt to pass a uniform law for six pilot towns had failed, and new attempts to pass a general law for all towns do not appear likely to succeed soon.

In all the towns I visited, intelligent plans, on the French model, had been prepared, but in none of them had any progress been made. Since these were the towns chosen for me by the national office concerned, and since very similar plans were in the operational stage in France, it appeared to me there was nothing we could learn from Italy which we could not learn better from France.

There was one exception to this: in Siena they had in operation a traffic restraint system which made it a pleasure to be in, walk around, and talk in the streets. It appeared to be universally popular and to be reasonably well observed (bearing in mind that the observance of regulations in Italy is more relaxed than in England).

I concluded that the problem in England, France and Italy was much the same. The threats were, and still are, decay and development in all three countries; too little economic activity in the old town centre, or too much. In the continental countries decay was the bigger threat, in England development, but that was only a matter of emphasis.

We obviously had much to learn from the French, but more, I thought, from the verve and comprehensiveness of their approach than from the actual procedures they adopted. The French scheme had grown since Mérimée out of their social and administrative structures, and ours must grow out of ours; they must grow out of the tradition which Lubbock and Curzon and my own father had left us. We had no prefects, none of those powerful extensions of central government who, in France, sit beside a local authority and guide and control all its proceedings. Even the permission to demolish a listed building, which in France had to be given by the central government, could in England be given by the local authority alone. It is true that if an English local authority refused permission, an appeal lay to the central government but, if it intended to grant permission, those who thought permission should not be granted could not appeal to the minister. They could only ask him in his mere discretion to make a 'default Building Preservation Order', an extremely cumbrous and troublesome action which he very seldom took.

The French system had two other characteristics which would prevent us copying it in England. One was that the rents in the *secteurs sauvegardés* were very much higher after the treatment than before, and working class people could not afford to come back to their old homes. Such a situation would be out of the question in England. The other was that the work itself was fabulously expensive; as far as we could see it worked out at about £1 million an acre. They had originally intended to treat forty acres a year in different towns but had, not surprisingly, been forced by economic circumstances to reduce the rate.[1]

Nevertheless I was attracted, as I think all who have studied the matter have been attracted, by the idea of increasing central government control at the expense of local government. Some English local councils were entirely uninterested, some even actively anxious to get rid of their architectural heritage in the interest of commercial development, new roads, and higher rateable values. But others were good and, if any were, all could be.

---

[1]Now, five years later, there is disappointingly little to show for the French programme. Individual beauties, yes; but no general revival of old towns.

So I quickly put these temptations to *dirigisme* behind
me. It was the age of devolution, the age of popular
participation in decisions; it would have been quixotic
and ineffective to try to stand against that tide, let alone
to swim in the opposite direction. We had to improve
the system without reducing the local authorities' sphere
of responsibility.

There was also the question of finance. To help stem
the loss of our architectural heritage, we still had only
£450,000 a year to be spent on grants on the advice of
the Historic Buildings Council. This was not much, and
I did not know whether to be charmed or infuriated
when I discovered from a parliamentary question put
down by Mr Ben Whitaker that we were spending twice
as much on the military staff at the Embassy in Washing-
ton, and seven times as much on military bands.

Where, then, to begin? Mr Duncan Sandys, the Chairman of the Civic Trust, which was the national body
grouping all the urban local amenity societies, had
recently secured time by ballot to introduce a private
member's bill into the House of Commons, and he
intended to make it a Civic Amenities Bill. He was
already in touch with Richard Crossman about this. Part
of the bill was to give local authorities powers to remove
bulky waste and old cars, and to set up disposal places
for these, and part was to be about preserving trees.
But the main part was to be about old towns. He was
himself a former minister of Housing and Local Government, so he knew his way round the government jungle.
Crossman decided he should have all the help possible
from our Department in drafting his bill, and there
emerged the new concept of the Conservation Area.

The Bill bound local authorities to designate these
conservation areas, and to use their planning powers to
'maintain and enhance' their historic and architectural
character. It did not bind them to use their highway and
transport powers to the same end, an omission which I
came to regret not having fought to rectify. Nor did it

give them any new powers or any new grants. This was a time—indeed we never got out of it during the Labour Government of 1964-70—of public economy and, as to powers, the civil service was still largely facing in the direction where the Conservatives had left them; new government powers, whether local or central, were to be strenuously avoided. So it seemed best to get the Civic Amenities Bill safely through, and then see what we could load onto it later.

After the Bill passed, in 1967, there was some discussion about what advice we should give the local authorities on designating their conservation areas. Some said we should urge them to settle their conservation policies first, and only then designate the areas in which they were to be applied. Others said we should urge them to designate their areas first, according to an objective assessment of what was worth 'conserving', and then decide the policies for doing it later. I favoured the latter course, since it was clear that public concern for historic towns and villages was going to go on increasing. I wanted the local authorities to designate many and large areas, which they probably would if they did so before thinking out what had to be done, and then apply increasingly energetic policies in them. If they first discovered how much had to be done and how troublesome it was all going to be, and only then began to designate the areas in the light of that newly acquired knowledge, they would no doubt designate more sparingly.

So we advised the local authorities to designate first and think later, and this, broadly speaking, is what they did. At the time of writing, about 1,350 conservation areas exist in about 130 local authority areas. Forty-one authorities have declared none. It is not simple to say who is 'doing best': if Kent have eighty-four and Hampshire thirty-five, that may be a Kentish preference for many and small rather than few and large. Hampshire's record in preservation is unassailable. It is easy to see who is doing badly, though: Durham, West Suffolk,

West Sussex with three each; Northumberland with two, Leicestershire and the North Riding with one, and bottom of all with a resounding nil comes Norfolk, whose market towns and villages round their mini-cathedrals are to common knowledge among the finest in Europe.

So much for the counties. Leading the County Boroughs is, of all places, Bolton, with eleven conservation areas. Liverpool and Nottingham have nine each, and Gloucester eight. But York, with four big ones, achieves just as full a cover. Of the numerous county boroughs with none, many may strike us as quite realistic. Barnsley, Salford, Wallasey. . . But Ipswich, Reading, Stockport; these are surprising.

Westminster heads the London Boroughs with fourteen; among the nil returns, Hammersmith is the most deplorable.

In 1971, a Bill was introduced into Parliament to give the local authorities a new power to prevent the demolition of any building, whether or not it is individually listed, in the conservation areas. This would bring us at last close to the French *zones protégés,* a position which preservationists have been trying to reach at least since 1912.

To back up the new concept of the conservation areas which, though statutory in form was at that time no more than hortatory in substance, we published in 1967 an illustrated book called *Preservation and Change.* This was an idea which grew out of Crossman's weekend conference in Cambridge; 'the Ministry's coffee-table book'. It sought to shed light on the fact that it was not only single buildings which could have architectural or historic interest, but also groups of buildings, street, quarters of towns, whole towns. The illustrations were apposite and effective, but the text was something of a committee job. The need to avoid alienating those local councillors on whose increased understanding we had to rely to get the job done was sometimes allowed to obscure the very points we ought to have made to them. But I

expect it did more good than harm, and much of the
material we did not put in it came out later under the
name of its real author, Roy Worskett.[1]

An estimate had now come in of the annual number
of listed buildings lost; it was 400 from the Statutory list
alone. The number from the supplementary list might
have been absolutely anything. This was pretty shocking;
I had hoped it would be less than that. Of course it might
be less; this was only the roughest guess since a local
authority could give permission without the ministry
ever knowing about it. But equally it might be more.
In any case, it was obviously quite unacceptable, and
I made an emotional speech about it in Chester, vowing
that we would get it down, and undertaking to come
back and tell them the new rate when we had it.

I chose Chester for this speech because it was one of
the five towns which Crossman had chosen for detailed
study after the Churchill College meeting, and because
it was the one among the five where they looked like
getting on with the job with the least fuss. We all knew
that we did not really know how to stop the pitiful and
unnecessary waste of those very civilised living environ-
ments, our old towns. So the best thing was to hire
qualified people from outside and ask them to find out.
Professor Colin Buchanan, the founder of modern urban
traffic studies, had already done a traffic study in Bath.
He is also an architect by training, and a former planning
inspector of the Ministry. So he was asked to study how
Bath could be preserved. Mr Donald Insall, a younger
man becoming well-known for his skilful and sensitive
restorations of old buildings, was chosen for Chester.
Lord Esher, the melancholy and euphonious chronicler
of architecture's attempts to meet and stem the decline
of civilisation, was asked to do York. Chichester would
not risk having an outside consultant, so we agreed that
if Mr G. S. Burrows, the County Planning Officer of

[1]Roy Worskett *The Character of Towns*, Architectural Press,
1969.

West Sussex, did the work, that would count. Miss Elizabeth Chesterton had recently made an outstanding study of part of Kings Lynn, and she was asked to undertake an overall study of how that splendid town could be preserved.

In each case the Ministry was to find half the cost. Bath and Chester, where the Councils had long become convinced that preservation was sound sense, agreed to fork out their respective halves, and Chichester went ahead under its own special arrangement. The City Council of York were reluctant, but fortunately York is a university city and has a strong local amenity society, the York Civic Trust, which offered to pay a quarter, and this shamed the Council into taking on the last quarter. But Kings Lynn proved a backwater in more than one sense, and nothing could be arranged there, so that study unhappily fell through.

There was a lot of discussion about the terms of reference for the studies, York City Council especially using every possible gambit to restrict Lord Esher's freedom to tell them they ought to be doing anything they were not already doing. But in the end the terms of reference were agreed; their more important provisions ran, with local variations, as follows:

1 The Consultant is asked to study and report on the implications of a conservation policy for the historic core of . . .

2 The primary object of the policy will be to preserve, and where possible enhance, the architectural and historic character of the area, in order to maintain its life and economic buoyancy.

3 The study should identify in detail the particular features—buildings, groups of buildings, street patterns, street scenes, spaces and other aspects of the selected area—which it is thought desirable to preserve, and should explain the reasons for the choice. It will also be necessary in some cases to consider the suitability of these buildings or groups of buildings to fulfil their present function or their adap-

tability where necessary to some other function.

4 The study should take account of the various practical problems which conservation is likely to encounter, including:

(a) motor traffic and car parking, covering both long-term solutions and interim remedial measures;

(b) commercial pressures on the area, and how they can be met without damaging its character, or alternatively how they can be accommodated elsewhere; for this purpose and as an aid to his study the Consultant will be supplied with copies of planning applications approved or under consideration relating to shopping, office and similar development.

5 The study should deal with:

(a) the preservation of listed buildings in the area, including the economics of restoration and maintenance, or where necessary, conversion to new uses. This will involve some consideration of the existing or proposed land uses within the area, and the amounts of accommodation likely to be required for different purposes in the future.

(b) the measures to be taken for environmental improvement in the area.

(c) the means to control any necessary new development to ensure that it is sympathetic to the environment both in design and quality.

(d) the total cost of conservation, including the public expenditure required and the programming of this expenditure, especially against the likely programming of relevant development outside the area, and other possible sources of revenue.

6 It will not be possible to consider the problems of the conservation area in isolation from the rest of the town and the Consultant will need to relate his proposals for that area to the current planning proposals for the town as a whole in consultation with the City Planning Officer; but if he finds it impossible so to relate his proposals in any instance he should say so and why.

7 Similarly, while the study will necessarily be carried out within the framework of existing legislation, the Consultant will be free to suggest any changes in the law which

seem to him to be necessary to secure an effective conservation policy.

I had been particularly insistent on paragraphs 6 and 7.

So the Four Towns Studies were commissioned in a reasonably auspicious way, and we now had to wait for years rather than months for the advice we needed.

One piece was missing, and that was advice on how to draw the lessons from the four samples of local detail and work them up into a national policy, which, in a matter like this, could only properly be undertaken in the light of these sample local details. The four consultants themselves were not asked to do this, though I think they could have been. The relevant officials in the Ministry were overworked anyhow, and I agreed with them that constructing new policies is not something that ought to be done by the officials whose lives are passed carrying out the old ones. There has to be some standing back. So Mr J. D. Jones, then our Deputy Secretary concerned with planning, suggested that I should gather a policy group to set about the job. Crossman accepted this suggestion. We invited Sir Nikolaus Pevsner, the doyen of architectural history in England, and many would say the man who introduced it into England; Mr Theo Crosby, an architect and designer whose ability to pick up a situation and shake it until the obvious truth dropped out I had long admired; Mr R. A. McCall, the Town Clerk of Winchester, a city with a preservation record as good as any in the country; Mr Alfred Wood, Planning Officer of the City of Norwich, who closed a historic shopping street to traffic in that city in a way that has since become a locus classicus of good planning; Mr H. J. Buck, a property consultant who had earlier worked in the Estates Branch of the Ministry; Professor Alan Day the economist, to remind us that short-term profit assessed by conventional accounting procedures is not the end of economic wisdom; Mr H. A. Walton, a planner with a special interest in villages, lent to us by the Kent

County Council; Mr Anthony Dale, who, as Chief Investigator, was responsible for drawing up the statutory lists of buildings of architectural and historic interest on which the whole edifice of preservation rested and whose levelheaded realism was more than equal to that task, and officials from the Ministries of Housing and Transport. The presence of Ministry of Transport officials in the Group, and the consequent commitment of that ministry to its recommendations, was a small epoch, unknown to the general public. The four consultants came to meetings when their reports were being discussed. I was the Chairman.

The terms of reference of the Group were:

(i) To co-ordinate the special studies of historic areas in five towns recently announced by the Minister, and to consider the results.

(ii) To review experience of action to preserve the character of other historic towns.

(iii) To consider measures adopted in other countries for preserving the character of historic towns and villages, and their effect.

(iv) To consider, in the light of the foregoing, what changes are desirable in current legal, financial and administrative arrangements for preservation, including the planning and development aspects, and to make recommendations.

This, then, was the point we had reached when, in the summer of 1966, George Brown's economic policy came to pieces, and it turned out that in spite of this his position in the Labour Party was still such that, when he thought the next job for him ought to be Foreign Secretary, the Prime Minister had to agree. This meant a general post in the Cabinet, and the occasion was taken to restore civilian rule in the House of Commons now that the martial law which had to be introduced when Labour was returned with a majority of three in 1964 was no longer necessary. The chief agent of civilian rule was to be Mr Crossman as Leader of the House, and Anthony Greenwood succeeded him as Minister of Housing and Local Government, which he remained until the Election of 1970, when he stood down from the House of Commons and became Lord Greenwood.

It may be of interest to pause here and mention the division of labour within the Ministry. The statutory powers belonged to the Minister and to him alone, as is always the case. Everything done by a junior minister or by what is increasingly called a 'middle-grade minister', namely a minister of state, or a minister with a fancy title but no department of his own, is done in the name of the departmental minister concerned. Parliament confers powers on ministers, and not many ministers at that. In statute law no-one exists except the Minister and, a hundred miles behind, the Permanent Secretary, who has statutory responsibilities limited to financial accounting only.

That is the framework of the matter, but of course different working relationships evolve between junior ministers and their bosses. Mr Greenwood was by nature a delegator, and left his junior ministers pretty free to develop policy about their own sectors, though he was himself far from uninterested in the sector of historic buildings and conservation since, like Mr Crossman, he is a cultivated person. Preservation is by statute part of planning law, and we had throughout the first part of my time in the Ministry a 'middle-grade minister' in charge of planning; Mr Willey at first, then Mr Niall McDermot and lastly, for a short time, Mr Kenneth Robinson. These too, and Mr McDermot most of all, were kind enough to leave preservation more or less in my hands.

The bottom layer, the parliamentary secretaries, passed jobs around according to fluctuating work loads and to the wish of the Minister. At one time I was developing policy towards the improvement of the older housing stock in general, and got out the White Paper on that subject in 1968, but thereafter left it. In time I accumulated a rather wide sector of work. For the last year or two of our time in office I was looking after the planning system as a whole and preservation within that; office development permits, advertisement control, air pollution, water pollution, beach pollution, noise, and the disposal of radioactive wastes; water supply, sewerage and sewage treatment; and public relations for the Ministry. This, especially with the great internal struggles necessary to get the Royal Commission on the Environment set up, and the office of the Secretary of State, and the Central Pollution Control Unit, and the Advisory Council on Noise, and the White Paper on the Pollution of the Environment, and all the other elements in the 'environmental revolution' in Whitehall of October 1969, made me spend less time than I would have liked on preservation pure and simple. Moreover, before that, there was a time when I was handling in the House of Lords the legislation and business not only of the Ministry of Housing and Local Government as a whole, but also of the Ministry of Technology and the Department of Health and Social Security, business which was handled in the House of Commons by eleven ministers. It is true, of course, that the House of Commons works harder than the House of Lords, but not eleven times harder. On the other hand, I had no constituency.

The main improvement in the system of preservation effected by the Labour Governments of 1964-70 was Part V of the Town and Country Planning Act of 1968. This Act, the second major reform and improvement of the great Planning Act of 1947 (the first one having been in 1962) introduced the modern system of local authority planning, with the Structure Plans, the Action Areas, and so on. Its origins in the Planning Advisory Group report of 1966, and its purposes and effects in general are well known, and need not detain us here.

Part V, on Buildings of Architectural or Historic Interest, is based on the work of the Preservation Policy

Group, done before the Four Towns Reports were received. Some of this work confirmed impressions and policies which had grown up earlier in the Ministry.

The 1968 Planning Act closed three major gaps in the law of preservation: the Silhill Gap, the Sick Typist Gap, and the Development Value Compensation Gap.

The first had been used to good effect by a man who became known to the press as the Vandal of Silhill. In 1966 the owner of a fine medieval manor house at Silhill near Solihull in the West Midlands was reported by the press to have said that he was going home one night past the manor house. He saw it flapping a bit in the wind and, since he had his bulldozer handy, he thought it safest to bring it along and knock the manor down. The manor, a listed building, was subject to a Provisional Building Preservation Order, and the offender was brought to justice. But, and this is the point, he could only be fined £100, this being then the maximum penalty on indictment. Now it so happened that The Vandal was a speculative housing developer, and the press reported him as saying that while he had only paid £15,000 for the old manor, the cleared site was worth £60,000 for building on.

So it was necessary to increase the penalties, and the 1968 Act increased them 'on summary conviction to imprisonment for a term of not more than three months or a fine of not more than £250 or both; or on conviction on indictment to imprisonment for a term not exceeding twelve months or an unlimited fine or both'; and provided that 'in determining the amount of any fine to be imposed on a person convicted on indictment, the court shall in particular have regard to any financial benefit which has accrued or appears likely to accrue to him in consequence of the offence.' There have been no Silhills since.

The Sick Typist Gap was this. Under the 1947 and 1962 Acts, the owner of a listed building did not have to have anyone's permission to demolish or alter it; he only had to have silence. It was his duty to inform the local authority of his intention to demolish or alter and, if within two months the local authority had not answered, or had answered asking for more information but without making any specific objection, he was free to carry out his intention. If the local authority did object it had to commence the Byzantine ritual of the Building Preservation Order, which had been modelled in 1947 on the old Preservation Order of the 1913 Ancient Monuments Act. It was an order not indeed prohibiting whatever action the owner had communicated his intention of taking (alteration or demolition) but assuming power over the building in such a way as later to be able to prohibit it. It had to be framed so as specifically to require the applicant to seek permission to do whatever he wanted to do. But the Local Authority could only make this order in a provisional form, and it would not come into effect until it had been confirmed by the Minister. The applicant had the right to lay before the Minister his objections to the provisional order being confirmed, and the Minister had to consider these. If after consideration he did confirm it, the applicant then had to request specific permission to do what he wanted to do and, if the Local Authority did not reply within two months, the applicant could take his permission for granted. If the Local Authority in due course refused permission, the applicant once again had a right of appeal to the Minister. This time his appeal would be against the refusal of the permission which the Minister's earlier rejection of his objections to the confirmation of the provisional order had obliged him to seek.

All stages of the procedure were a lawyer's paradise, and at all of them typists could be away sick, thus nullifying the whole. Its complications were such that local authorities seldom undertook it in the first place, and on the few occasions when they brought it to a successful conclusion the status of the 'order building' at the end

of the day was a statutory sore thumb, something extraordinary which, by the force of language and the irrita-
tion of experience, was felt to be an imposition or even
a little tyranny. The weakest point in the chain was the
onus on the local authority to take the first positive
action of making a provisional order within two months.
Not only if a typist was sick, but also if a letter went
astray, if a council official was not quite familiar with all
the red tape, or if, being familiar, he was hesitating to
enter the maze, the building could be lost. I guessed a
good part of the 400 a year were slipping through this
gap.

The 1968 Act therefore abolished the Building Preservation Order altogether, and made it necessary for the
owner to have, once and for all, the express permission
of the local authority or, on appeal, of the Minister,
before he could demolish or alter a listed building. If
the local authority did not reply to an application within
a period—of six months instead of the earlier two—the
owner was to take his application as having been refused,
instead of allowed as under the earlier law, and could
then appeal direct to the Minister.

The Development Value Compensation Gap, being
even more complicated and Byzantine, was, if anything,
an even bigger deterrent to local authorities doing anything under the old law. It was this. If at the end of the
day a Building Preservation Order had been made to
stick, it was open to the owner to claim that he had
thereby been deprived of reasonable beneficial use of his
land, and, if he could sustain this claim, he could compel
the local authority to buy it from it. (This is one of the
few examples in our planning law of compulsory purchase in reverse.) Now most of the loss of listed buildings
was at this time happening in the squares and high
streets of our historic towns, and it was happening
because large commercial interests, chain stores and
office developers, wanted advantageous sites for new
buildings. Since they were large and prosperous, they

had good lawyers who could see to the end of the game
before they began. But advantageous sites were precisely
those town-centre sites where the differential between
existing use value (leaving the old house standing) existing use development value (demolishing the old house
and building a new house) and change of use development value (demolishing the old house and building a
supermarket or office block) was widest. Those were the
very sites where they could make most money. But the
old law said that if, after he had been refused permission
to demolish, the owner succeeded in making his purchase
notice stick (and this too had to be confirmed by the
Minister) then the local authority was bound to buy the
building at the full change-of-use development value;
that is, it was bound to compensate the owner for not
being allowed to build his office block or supermarket.

Now the local authorities also had good lawyers who
were able to see to the end of the game. The game
consisted of six or seven moves on each side: twelve or
fourteen moves in all. If the developer won, he got his
profitable development. If he lost he stood a very good
chance of being compensated to the tune of what he
would have gained if he had won. If the local authority
won, it ran a correspondingly high risk of having to lay
tens of thousands, perhaps hundreds of thousands, of
pounds on the rates for the pleasure of keeping a nice
old building. Even if it avoided that, it had the certainty
of weeks of hard legal and administrative work by people
who could be better employed. If it lost, all that happened was one listed building the less and one commercial development the more. Why start on a mug's game
in the first place?

I decided therefore that we must do two things: first,
we must make it clear that 'reasonable beneficial use'
meant virtually any beneficial use, and not simply a use
which was less beneficial than the intended new development. That we put in a circular under the 1968 Act. The
other was that the local authority must not be forced to

pay any development value at all if it had at the end of
the day to buy a preserved building, but only the value
of that building as it then stood for its existing use. I
did not see why society should compensate big developers
for not spoiling our towns any more than it compensated
shopworkers for not robbing the till or, a closer analogy,
any more than it compensated the very same big
developers when they were refused planning permission
to build on green field sites.

My suspicion that this proposal went to the heart of
the matter was confirmed in a strange way by the reaction
it provoked. It landed me in the second biggest internal
fight of my years in the government; (the biggest was
over the setting up of the Royal Commission on the
Environment). The fight lasted eight months. As I was
then still largely ignorant of the solicitude of the civil
service for property interests, my first move was to ask
our officials for figures about the amounts actually paid
out in development value compensation by local authorities forced to acquire listed buildings under the law as
it stood. This they agreed to do, but never did. Next I
sought the opinion of the Preservation Policy Group,
which endorsed the proposal along with various others.
I therefore chose it from the general list of suggestions
for inclusion in the Planning Bill which was then being
prepared.

At that point I received the first objections from the
departmental officials. They were in unco-ordinated
form, so I co-ordinated them, weighed them against the
advantages, decided they were outweighed, and so
informed the officials. I next received from them a set
of co-ordinated objections, more or less identical with
those I had sent to them. The major thread of their
case was simply that it was unfair to deprive people of
their property rights; the minor that even if big
developers were not allowed development value, small
and ignorant people ought to be, because they had not
consciously been pursuing it; the widows and orphans

argument. I told the senior official concerned that I fully understood the case, considered it not without weight, but believed it was overridden by the contrary case for changing the law. My own decision was still the same.

I supposed the next step would be to take the disagreement to the Minister (Mr Greenwood) and very much wondered which of us would persuade him. But the officials tried another gambit; they submitted to me for onward transmission to him a paper on all the things which ought to go into the Preservation part of the Planning Bill, which not only did not set out the pros and cons of this proposal, but did not mention it at all. I disapproved the paper, and asked that it come forward again, including a section setting out the pros and cons of changing the compensation law. Shortly after that I learned that the paper I had disapproved had gone to the Minister. I informed him of my disapproval, and of the reasons for it and at the same time asked the senior official concerned whether the Department would now produce a paper for the minister discussing this matter and setting out the pros and cons of the course proposed. I was informed they would not.

This was dramatic. I was now faced with the choice of continuing to make a stink within the Ministry, complaining of the official concerned to the Permanent Secretary, informing the Minister that I was being prevented from doing my job, etc., etc., or of making a tactical deviation. The former course would have been time-consuming, adrenalin-releasing, and probably unavailing. As Chairman Mao teaches us, the big battalions are best not tackled head on by a junior minister. So I decided to seek the legal and professional help I needed from outside the Civil Service. I was just picking up the phone to do so when the official in question returned, and said the Department would, on second thoughts, prepare the paper that was needed.

This had taken four months so far, and there was just time for a short rest if we were to catch the Bill.

Two months later we resumed; a fair paper setting out the pros and cons was considered at a meeting of ministers and officials chaired by Mr Willey, since compensation for the public purchase of property as such was in his sphere of action. The meeting decided the thing should be done. We used at that time to have a meeting every Monday morning of all the ministers in the department, followed by one between all the ministers and the top half dozen or so officials. At the next Monday morning 'ministers and officials', this decision was reported and endorsed, and a few weeks later a technical paper arrived from the compensation branch of the Ministry setting out how the change could be made in terms of statute law and current legal and administrative practice. We now seemed to be back on the rails.

But the administrators shot one more bolt; the next one up the ladder from my last antagonist wrote a paper saying how difficult it all was, and that we should not do it. I minuted simply that the matter was decided, and I was against reopening it. Nevertheless, Mr Willey sent it all over to our legal branch for further clarification, and it looked as though we might yet come unstuck.

And so it might have been but for the fact that because of all this in-fighting the historic building section of the bill had fallen behind the others in preparation. It therefore had to go separately to the relevant Cabinet committee for endorsement of the policy by the government as a whole, the rest having already been endorsed. Since this was the historic buildings part of the bill, it fell to my lot to steer it through the Cabinet committee. The paper prepared at official level for this meeting had been cast, whether by a careless enemy or by a cunning friend I never knew, in a form which made no mention of the contentious provision at all, but simply ended up by stating that a verbal report would be made on various minor changes proposed in the law. There were four such changes; I gave a full and clear account of each of them, including this compensation matter, and the committee endorsed them all without discussion.

Parliament equally, which I had been informed would be most reluctant to deprive the citizen of his property rights in this way, showed itself quite unconcerned at the rectification of an anomaly which certainly not more than two or three members ever knew existed, and there was no discussion of the matter in either House. The Act as passed provided that when the owner of a preserved building compelled the local authority to buy it as being no longer of reasonable beneficial use, and the local authority thought the owner had been letting it decay in order to obtain the development value of the site, the local authority could apply to the Minister for a direction that they should pay no development value in the price for this building. The owner could take the local authority to court if he wished to dispute the fact that he had purposely let his building decay. The bit about purposely allowing the building to decay in order to obtain development value I had been talked into by the widows and orphans argument. It is probably all right, because to the extent it stops developers deliberately allowing listed buildings to decay, it presumably makes it less likely they can claim no reasonable beneficial use from them. So this provision stopped up another of the main leaks in the law through which listed buildings were being lost, brought it into line with French and Italian law and, what is more important, with justice and common sense.

The 1968 Planning Act introduced a whole host of minor improvements. It explicitly allowed the Minister's investigators to list a building because of its contribution to a group of buildings; it included anything fixed to a building in the listing, thus preventing the former habit of removing and selling off woodwork, clocks, etc., without planning permission; and it laid the Minister and the local authorities under the positive duty of having special regard to the desirability of preserving a listed building when called upon to decide a case. This last may seem odd, but there were in fact lawyers ready to challenge the propriety of taking this into account under the old law. The old law only required notice to be given, etc., if the proposed alteration 'seriously' affected the character of the listed building. The 1968 Act got rid of that 'seriously', and spoke of alterations or extensions which would 'in any manner' affect its character. The implication of this is that the 10% increase in the volume of a building, which allows people to make small additions to ordinary houses without permission, the so-called 'ten per cent tolerance', does not apply to listed buildings. The Act also provided that if permission is granted to demolish, the Royal Commission on Historical Monuments must have time to record the building photographically before it goes. It provided that consents to demolish, unlike other planning permissions, might be limited to one person. It made local authorities apply to the Minister for consent to demolish their own listed buildings, instead of giving it to themselves as formerly. It provided that local authorities must not allow demolitions or alterations without consulting such amenity societies as the Minister might specify, and these are at present the Ancient Monuments Society, the Council for British Archaeology, the Society for the Protection of Ancient Buildings, the Georgian Group, the Victorian Society, and the Royal Commission on Historical Monuments. This built these excellent and hitherto somewhat neglected bodies right into the law. It required local authorities to advertise all the more important applications to alter or demolish listed buildings, and to stick notices on the buildings themselves in order to give local opinion time to bear on the issue. It also made them stick up notices about all planning applications in or affecting a Conservation Area. It required them to inform the Minister when they were minded to give permission, so he could consider whether to call the application in for his own decision, generally so as to have a public local enquiry. It empowered local authorities to require owners of listed buildings to repair them and, if they did not, compulsorily to purchase the building for the purpose of preservation. (This provision was carefully dovetailed with the reverse procedure under which the owner compels the local authority to purchase the building, and gets no development value compensation if he has neglected it on purpose.) More, it provided that if the owner wrongfully demolished his listed building, the site could still be acquired compulsorily, and it extended all this procedure to buildings owned by the local authorities themselves, so that the Minister now stands in the same relationship to the local authority as the local authority does to a private owner. It gave local authorities proper powers to enforce the undoing of alterations carried out without permission, or to undo them itself and recover the cost, and it codified the rights of appeal against all these decisions. It gave the local authorities a new power to serve a Building Preservation Notice (not to be confused with the rare, onerous, and now extinct, Building Preservation Order) on the owner of an unlisted building which it thinks ought to be listed, and this lasts for six months while the Minister considers whether to list it.

Under a private member's Act introduced, as we have seen, by Mr Paul Channon in 1962, local authorities might make grants from their own funds for the repair of listed buildings, and of unlisted buildings with the Minister's consent. The 1968 Act made it unnecessary for them to have the Minister's consent in respect of unlisted buildings.

About this time, I had a good look at what one might call the surrounding landscape. One more small thing we did to supplement and reinforce the work of the voluntary bodies. The Society for the Protection of Ancient Buildings had for some time run a service to help prospective buyers and sellers of such buildings to meet each other. Building on a spare-time enterprise set up by a Ministry of Works surveyor, we established within the Ministry of Housing a Historic Buildings Bureau, which publishes a periodical sheet with details of listed buildings for sale, and where intending purchasers of such buildings can enquire if there is anything that suits them. A building must have been on the market for two months before it gets onto the Historic Buildings Bureau's books and, in order not to do ordinary estate agents out of part of their living, the Bureau makes no charge for its services.

Another and more important thing we did was to get rid of Grade III on the list. It had become increasingly clear that there was not much point in listing buildings in a way that had no legal force. So we decided that during the second round of listing (the Investigators having by then covered the whole country for the first time) about half the Grade III buildings should be up-graded to Grade II on the statutory list, and the rest would be notified by the Chief Investigator of historic buildings to the local authorities as of local interest. In order to make it clear exactly what this means, I reproduce in an appendix, with the agreement of the Chief Investigator of Buildings of Historic and Architectural Interest, the documents which, taken together, constitute present listing policy. They are rather long, but many people are puzzled about how all this works, and these hitherto unpublished texts are of interest.

The voluntary societies were now built into the legal procedures by the Act itself, and we should have to wait and see how that system worked out. But what of the various statutory bodies? The oldest was the Royal Commission on Historical Monuments. It had set out sixty years previously to investigate and publish all the buildings of interest built before a certain date. The date had been advanced first to 1714 and then, in 1962, to 1855. Even before this increase in the field to be covered, progress was monumentally slow; it was now glacier-like. Slowness, it is true, is the proper concomitant of excellence, and the recent volumes about the cities of Oxford and Cambridge with their magnificent photographs had perhaps set a new standard to the world in how these things should be done. The sideline volumes, like the one about the Civil War siege works at Newark, were also highly valuable and interesting.

But slowness was still a worry. There was in circulation a joyful paper by Sir Nikolaus Pevsner on how the Commission's work could be speeded up so as to finish, not in 500 years, which it would at its present speed, but in 300. I never heard that the Pevsner proposals were adopted. Moreover, the Commission cost about £30,000 a year, and this seemed to me a lot to be spending on recording the buildings, when we only had half a million to preserve them. Indeed, if we went on losing listed buildings at the rate of 400 a year, they would all be gone in 250 years, and the last parts of the country would still have another two hundred and fifty years to wait before the Commission got round to recording where they had been. So it occurred to me to think of distributing the work of the Royal Commission among the universities of England, many of which have first rate departments of architectural history or the equivalent, in such a way as to ensure that no work which was being done by the Commission remained undone, or was worse done. This might speed it up and, even allowing for Government financial priming for the new system, might free some funds to staunch that 400 a year. But the Commission was the responsibility of the Treasury; suggestions were lobbed to and fro in a rhythm hardly less relaxed than the Commission's own, and nothing came of it. Perhaps it was as well.

The Royal Fine Arts Commission had been set up in 1924 to give advice to any public body which sought it, on the look of proposed new buildings. It was potentially a useful body, but it had two drawbacks. The first was that many of the most prolific architects in the country were members, and it naturally seldom criticised the work of its own members. There was a foolish system by which, when a member's work was being judged, he retired temporarily from the room and returned for the next item on the agenda. Who this was supposed to impress, I am not sure. On the other hand, it was hard to think of another way of manning it. If its membership were to be limited to critics and historians of architecture, people would say: 'Those who can, do; those who can't may well have to be allowed to teach, but for heaven's sake don't let's have them giving statutory advice.' If, instead of the busiest architects, one appointed less busy ones, people would say it was the second best judging the best.

Its other drawback was its insuperable aversion from actually getting stuck in. It could give opinions when asked and, since 1933, when it was not asked. Moreover, under an admirable new system introduced in 1946, it could even send for papers and persons. So its opinions were often first rate. But would it go along and defend them at a public enquiry? Never. Its opinions were therefore shot down time and again by the opposition, usually big developers, on points which they were able, in the absence of argument, to make seem important, but which were not so. I tried more than once, with successive chairmen, to get them to back up their written opinions with a personal presence at enquiries, but my attempts always failed because the written opinions were highest common factors, not more than one member could reasonably be expected to go to an enquiry, and there was no one member who could be trusted by the others not to go beyond the highest common factor. It would be invidious, and perhaps improper, to go into details, but if the plans for the future of Canterbury are not quite as good as they might be, it may be partly due to this reluctance.

Then there was the Historic Buildings Council, a statutory body which advised the Minister of Housing on how to spend, at that time, half a million a year on grants to the owners of listed buildings. It also has a committee to advise the Investigators on criteria for listing buildings. The Council was throughout my time chaired by Lord Hailes, a former Conservative Whip, and its Listing Committee by Lord Holford, the architect and planner. From Lord Hailes I learned something of personal importance to me, namely that I had been doctrinaire and lacking a sense of reality in supposing, as I had, that the chairman of committees such as these ought to be people with a professional qualification for the job. If they were not, I had thought they ought to be apolitical, or at least they ought not to be that most political of all animals, a whip. In fact the work of the Committee was done throughout my time (though with the help, it must be admitted, of two outstanding civil servants as secretary) expertly, sensitively, correctly, and without any hidebound fuss.

It was not through any feeling that it was doing wrong that I wanted changes, but because I conceived of a new role for state aid to the great country houses. Houses like Woburn and Beaulieu were magnificently preserved and gave pleasure to many millions of people from all over the world without their owners ever having received a penny from the state, while certain other houses, the owners of which were not notably less rich than Lord Montagu, and who had moreover received grants from the state, were being lost. The reason was that the Duke of Bedford and Lord Montagu understood what was now in effect a very large new business, and the others did not. Could we not help the others to understand it and make their houses pay for themselves? I thought perhaps we could, by slanting the Historic Buildings Council towards people with experience of the tourist trade, and later by linking the grants we might pay the owners of great houses, to their acceptance of advice on how to run them so as to break even. I secured the appointment of the Chairman of the Historic Houses Committee of the British Tourist and Holidays Association as a first step, and still hope that things may develop in this way.

I did not and do not share the distaste of some people for what has happened at Woburn and Beaulieu. It seems to me that Woburn is now an admirable social phenomenon. The children's amusements and the free-range zoo are interesting and enjoyable in the highest degree, the fine sweep of parkland and the setting of the house are no whit impaired by their presence, and there inside the house, because of the imagination that has gone into arranging what happens outside, the Duke is enabled to continue being a Duke to the top of his bent, eating off gold plate with hordes of relatives, friends and visitors, exactly as his ancestors did, exactly as our ancestors expected them to do, and exactly as we expect him to do. Only glum extremists, whether of right or of left, will complain at that.

During 1968 I was largely occupied with developing the new policy towards the 'old housing stock', namely the many millions of ordinary houses of no architectural or historic interest, which had been built before about 1920; in short, 'Coronation Street'. We had carried out a national survey of their condition and what they had in them in the way of bathrooms, water closets, etc., a survey a good deal more sophisticated and reliable than any before, and it had returned an answer of alarming gravity, the details of which fall outside the scope of this book. So we gathered another weekend conference, also at Cambridge, but this time at New Hall, of representatives from the local authorities, building societies, housing societies, the building industry, universities, and the press, to thrash out what ought to be done. To be more accurate, perhaps, it was to make sure that there were no possible solutions which we did not have before us in making our choice. I was the Chairman.

The main finding of the conference, and the main purpose of the Act which it engendered, was to rectify the imbalance in the grant levels between the improvement of old housing and the building of new. If a local authority found itself with a number of sad old houses which had twenty years more life structurally, it could choose between on the one hand improving them with bathrooms and their streets with trees, thus making them tolerable to live in, and on the other, achieving tolerable living conditions on the same land by knocking them down and building new housing now. Twenty years housing time by improvement, or sixty years by development? It was a sum, and the grants at that time were heavily loaded so that the sum almost always added up to redevelopment. We were thus losing a lot of old houses which could be redeemed, and, conversely, we were wasting a lot of building industry capacity and building money on replacing them, which should have gone on replacing irredeemable slums of which, God knows, there were and still are enough to be going on with.

The economic calculations we needed were mainly and, I thought very ably, done by Mr Lionel Needleman.

The existing clearance and redevelopment powers of housing authorities were also somewhat monolithic and tended towards the bulldozer approach. Housing authorities needed powers which would allow them to pick their way green-fingered through a part of their town, redeveloping here, improving there, all on a really sensitive, fine mesh. And these powers we proposed to give them in the new areas to be called General Improvement Areas.

So we got out a White Paper on all that, and Mr Greenwood's Housing Act of 1969 raised the general level of discretionary grants for these older houses by two and a half times. (The Ministry officials had wanted to raise them by a factor of two, I by a factor of three. Mr Greenwood split the difference.) During the first year in which the Act operated (1970) these provisions nearly doubled the rate of house improvement throughout the country. These house improvement grants, the General Improvement Areas, and the new powers and Exchequer grants for 'environmental improvement' (meaning pedestrianisation, trees, play spaces, and so on) are obviously of considerable incidental help to historic towns and villages.

The Four Towns Reports now began to come in. They naturally showed different emphases. At Bath, Professor Buchanan had made some broad recommendations about the historic part of the town as a whole, which is of course very large, and had then gone on to detailed and practical advice to the City Council about exactly what ought to be done with one small area for priority action. His recommendation dovetailed with what he had earlier recommended for roads and traffic, including his major and bold solution of a tunnel right under the hill. And this, indeed, remains the key to the preservation of Bath. A finding which was surprising to me and perhaps to many outsiders was how much of Bath the Council already owned.

Donald Insall had concentrated on the physical problems of Chester, and had come up with detailed and ingenious solutions to the problem of the intricate multiple ownership which zigzags, often vertically, through the Rows.

Oddly enough Mr Burrows, the Planning Officer of West Sussex, whom Chichester had chosen for safety's sake, came up with the proposals most cavalier towards property rights. In his chosen sector of study, one of the Pallants, as the old quarters of Chichester are called, he recommended an extremely bold and forward plan for compulsory public ownership which involved an unprecedented element of compulsion to be exercised by the majority of freeholders in an area against a minority which might not be willing to agree. This we found in the Preservation Policy Group to be altogether too novel and alarming to be recommended for general adoption, though no doubt if the local authority thought fit to try a private bill in due course, Parliament might agree.

The distinctive proposal in Lord Esher's plan for York was the suggestion of a local tax to be levied in shops and restaurants and devoted to preservation. Again, a private bill would presumably be the best way of getting this off the ground, if the Council wanted to. He also suggested an ingenious and far-reaching plan of controlled access for traffic of different kinds through the different gates of the walled city.

If we were to get in the wealth of photographs and maps the consultants had provided, the reports had to be published at seven pounds for each of the four volumes. This high price was much criticised and was to be regretted, but I had consulted commercial publishers and learned that the price would be about the same if it were published by any one other than the Stationery Office, so we just had to put up with it. It did not prove possible, either, to interest a commercial publisher in a simplified cheap edition of all four reports.

The Preservation Policy Group then got to work to draw the general lessons. All four consultants agreed that preservation was going to cost money. All four agreed that traffic was one of the main troubles, since the best use for an old house is the one it was built for, namely for people to live in, but you cannot expect people to live with mammoth lorries roaring and earthquaking past a few inches from the bedroom windows and sometimes knocking bits off the house. Therefore ringroads, ringroads, and more ringroads. And ringroads far enough out not to plough up the pleasant suburbs which many historic towns have, or the cathedral meadows, or whatever it might be. And the further out the more expensive.

The Preservation Policy Group's Report was ready in the winter of 1969-70, and the most important passage in it (paras 88-92) went as follows. We recommended:

That pilot projects be carried out in the four towns to see what can be done by a concerted use of existing powers in improving areas in historic towns. We think local authorities generally have the necessary powers to carry out these schemes. What local authorities will need are the staff to identify the areas where such schemes are to be carried out, to make a careful and detailed survey of what needs to be done, and how it should be done (bearing in mind that the planning of these areas must be related to the planning of the town as a whole and that it will also be necessary to decide what should be done first). Many of the costs of such schemes can be met with the help of existing Government grants. The fabric of historic houses can be repaired with the help of town scheme grants under the Historic Buildings and Ancient Monuments Act 1953, and they can be provided with modern amenities with grants under the Housing Act 1969—this Act also provides for grant towards general improvement of the surroundings and, indeed in some cases a housing improvement area may be also the right area for the sort of exercise we have in mind. Some road schemes attract grants, and so does the provision of additional public open space. The pilot projects will provide useful information on what powers and grants can be used for this purpose. Many of the services to be provided in historic towns would have to be provided in any case, even though they are not revenue producing, and, in the long term, conservation may well, by adapting buildings for new or renewed uses and by attracting tourists, produce an economic return.

Good estate management has a vital part to play here, and we believe the development by local authorities of a sound policy of estate management in its widest sense, understood by owners and occupiers alike so as to obtain their maximum co-operation, would constitute a major contribution towards successful conservation in a town. At least one of the four reports comments unfavourably on the fragmentation of legal interests, the divided responsibility for repairs, the lack of inspection, failure to enforce covenants in leases and the lack of interest in those parts of a building which cannot be lucratively occupied, in disregard of the damaging effect on the whole. These faults result from failure to apply sound policies of estate management. We see such a policy embracing the use of appropriate covenants in the sale and lease of land, the operation of planning or landlord's control to prevent the introduction of undesirable uses and to ensure that development and redevelopment contribute to the overall scheme of conservation, the acquisition of selected properties for renovation and conversion, the administration of grants to induce the repair and conversion of premises where this would not occur by normal economic processes, the improvement of the environment by the local authority under recent legislation, and the attraction of private finance for development and conservation wherever this is possible. The more extensive the ownership of property by local authorities within the historic centres of towns, the more effective will such policies be.

Nevertheless initial costs may be heavy, and there may be a net loss, at least in the early years of the conservation programme. The prospect of even a small overall loss might deter local authorities and, even more, private enterprise, from embarking on works of conservation. This problem is not peculiar to conservation: it is also met in the redevelopment of central areas where Exchequer grant is available for meeting part, usually half, of the approved net annual deficiency.

Perhaps the greatest lesson of the Four Towns Reports is that an analagous grant is required for conservation. It seems to us anomalous that redevelopment should be encouraged in this way, but not conservation. We also think that such a grant would encourage a comprehensive approach to conservation.

We therefore propose that local authorities should be encouraged to produce comprehensive schemes for the conservation of selected areas. The authority would calculate the receipts from all sources, including rents, rates and government grants, and set them against its estimated expenditure, which again would take into account all forms of conservation activity (including grants from its own funds, acquisition costs, costs of works and the cost of a conservation section on its own staff). Any deficit would then be calculated over an agreed period, say twenty years, and the Government would help the local authority with a grant towards the deficiency, perhaps at the rate of half the average annual deficiency for the period, after which the situation would be reviewed. We do not think, on the evidence of the Four Towns Reports, that the Government contribution would need to be large compared with other kinds of Government expenditure; and the power to approve the details and area of the schemes would give control over the extent of Government liability. But we think that a Government offer to share any loss with the ratepayers would give comprehensive conservation schemes just that initial stimulus which would enable them to get off the ground in our most important historic towns.

Our recommendations starting with the kepstone of the whole thing, the new General Conservation Schemes and the Exchequer grant for them, were as follows:

1 Legislation should be introduced to enable local authorities who submit a new type of General Conservation Schemes to be paid Exchequer grant to meet fifty per cent of the deficiency on their operation.

2 Pilot Schemes of this nature should be carried out immediately in advance of legislation, in Bath, Chester, Chichester and York.

3 The annual grants and loans to the owners of outstanding historic houses made by the Minister of Housing and Local Government on the advice of the Historic Buildings Council should be increased substantially beyond the present figure of £575,000, to enable both more individual houses to be assisted and more town schemes to be undertaken.

4 The possibility of an exchequer subsidy towards local authority expenditure on the repair of listed buildings not included in Town Schemes or General Conservation Schemes should be considered.

5 The possibility of introducing legislation so that the Government may guarantee advances made by building societies on the security of historic buildings should be considered.

6 Local planning authorities should be given power to charge the owner when they themselves repair listed buildings.

7 Existing legislation should be amended so that if an owner deliberately neglects a listed building in order to realise its break-up value the local authority may acquire

the building at a price which excludes the break-up value element.

8 The importance of preserving historic towns and areas should be given proper weight when considering the priority of road improvements and new roads.

9 The Ministry of Housing and Local Government and the Ministry of Transport should prepare a series of technical bulletins on street furniture, car parks, traffic management, Article 4 directions[1] and the re-use of old materials etc.

10 The English Tourist Board should be invited to take whatever steps are open to them to ensure the production of guide books to historic towns.

11 The Ministry of Housing and Local Government should issue a series of booklets, designed for a wide audience.

Here, I thought, and still think, was a comprehensive programme, suited to the fabric of British local and central government, and really likely to stop the rot and give us historic towns which were neither ruins nor museums, but once again living and pleasing places for living and conscious people.

The weather was still very bad on the government finance front. It already seemed likely that we should have an early election, in the spring of 1970. And I was heavily preoccupied with the White Paper on the Control of Pollution. But I set off on the battle to get funds, supported by a very small but by now really dedicated staff of officials directly concerned with the matter. The bid had to take its place with all the others on the Ministry of Housing shopping list, and many were the

---

[1]*Author's footnote:* An Article 4 direction is a direction which a local authority may ask the Minister to make in its favour, giving it the power to demand and determine planning applications in respect of a whole range of small works, (painting, fences, etc.) which are otherwise exempt from planning control.

twists and turns which were necessary. Mr Greenwood was favourable, but had to balance this one against several others. The Chancellor of the Exchequer, Roy Jenkins, was also favourable, but had to balance it against very many others indeed.

Known public opinion was strongly favourable, and the press, with the exception of an uncharacteristic leader in *The Times* on 23 July, 1966, had been unanimous all along that something like this ought to be done.

We won through, and on 20 May, 1970, I was able to announce that the Government accepted the report as a whole and in detail. On that day I made the following answer to a written question from Lord Faringdon in the House of Lords:

The Preservation Policy Group was appointed in June, 1966, under my chairmanship, to consider what changes were desirable in current legal, financial and administrative arrangements for the preservation of buildings of historic and architectural interest. Much of the advice given by the Group has already been taken into account in the new system of control over listed buildings introduced by Part V of the Town and Country Planning Act 1968, and in various improvements administrative practice. Our Report, which is now completed, deals principally with finance, but also reviews developments in preservation since 1966. In view of its interest, my right honourable friend the Minister of Housing and Local Government is arranging for it to be printed for publication in the summer. Copies will be available in the Library of both Houses next week.

The Group recommended a substantial increase in the amount of grants made on the advice of the Historic Buildings Council for individual outstanding buildings and for 'town schemes'. We also propose an Exchequer grant for historic areas which are to be the subject of a new type of general conservation scheme prepared by local authorities. This grant would meet half any net annual loss incurred by the authority on an approved scheme.

The Government accept the Report. As a first step, the amount of grants which the Historic Buildings Council can recommend has been increased from £575,000 to

£700,000 in the current financial year. At an early opportunity the Government will introduce legislation to enable
the payment of the proposed new grant on general conservation schemes. It is impossible to forecast precisely how
expenditure would run under these proposals, but my right
honourable friend would regard a gradual increase up
to a figure of £1½ million in 1973-74 as an acceptable rate.

In the meantime, I am today inviting the local authorities
in Bath, Chester, Chichester and York to discuss with me
the possibility of joining in carrying out pilot general
conservation schemes in those cities which were the subject
of the Four Towns Report.

The pilot schemes in the four cities were to be carried
out in advance of legislation, and we had Treasury
agreement to their being financed as to 50% from the
Exchequer, as the generality of schemes would later be
under the projected legislation.

The announcement went virtually unnoticed, since the
press was already occupied with the forthcoming general
election. Labour lost that election, and the decision to
introduce the grant-aided General Conservation Schemes,
the keystone of the whole arch and the main fruit of four
years work by all those best qualified in the field, was
reversed by the new Conservative Government. The publication of the Report itself was postponed from the
summer of 1970 till January 1971. On January 1 Mr
Peter Walker, the Secretary of State for the Environment,
sent it to local authorities under cover of a circular which
said in part:

The Group also recommend legislation to enable local
authorities who submitted a new type of general conservation scheme to be paid Exchequer grant to meet 50 per
cent of the deficiency on their operation. The Government
consider that a decision on this recommendation would be
premature until the pilot projects have been carried further.
The decision will need to take account of the Government's
desire to give local authorities greater financial freedom
and responsibility.

The last sentence contained the message. 'To give local authorities greater financial freedom and responsibility' is a widely understood euphemism for cutting Exchequer grants and throwing everything back on the rates. In the case of preservation, this is a more than usually inequitable thing to do since some local authorities have many hundreds or, in the case of counties, even thousands of listed buildings to look after, while others have just about none.

But there was worse. The 'decision' which the circular said would be 'premature' had in fact, as we have seen, already been taken by the preceding Government seven months earlier. The circular thus sought to avoid the plain language of truth, which would have been unpopular. The language of truth would have said: 'The Government hereby reverses the decision of its predecessor, and cancels the committed expenditure on these new schemes, namely £1½ million a year by 1973-4, to be matched by an equal amount from the local authorities, making £3 million a year in all'.

After tacitly reversing the main decision of the former Government, the circular went on to reaffirm its acceptance of the minor recommendations in the report, including the minor financial one, namely that the Historic Buildings Council's normal grants should run at the higher rate of £700,000 a year. In the summer of 1971 the present Government raised this sum again, to £1 million a year, an increase of £300,000 a year, or exactly one tenth of the increase they had cancelled on January 1.

In November 1971 the Government introduced a Town and Country Planning (Amendment) Bill which contained preservation clauses,[1] but did not embody any of the minor recommendations of the Kennet Report. To neglect such an opportunity of legislating seemed to cast doubt on the statement in the circular of 1 January 1971, that these minor recommendations were still accepted.

[1] See p. 67.

All in all, 1 January 1971 was a bad day for British preservation law and policy.

Two important issues remain to be discussed: the Land Fund, and Churches in Use.

We have seen how when Hugh Dalton was Chancellor of the Exchequer in the first post-war Labour Government, he set up a new Land Fund, designed to enable the state to acquire, in lieu of death duties, fine old buildings and pictures, and amenity land, for the general good. A few such acquisitions were made by the Conservative governments of 1951-64, but by the time I came on the scene the strong dislike of it evinced by Treasury officials had long since caused it to fall into abeyance. The Land Fund had been reduced in size, and was in perpetual danger of being altogether extinguished. The original Act gave the government power not only to buy direct, but also to grant-aid purchases by local authorities. This last power had never been used. We used it for the first time to spend £100,000 on the repair and reinstatement of Gainsborough Old Hall in Lincolnshire, which had been given to the Minister for the public, and we revived the main power with the purchase of Heveningham Hall in 1969.

Heveningham Hall is a fine large eighteenth-century house in a singularly inaccessible part of Suffolk. The current owner, wishing to emigrate to Australia, played a wholly intransigent hand with the government to get the best possible price for his asset. He secured lawyers highly capable of seeing to the end of the game, and carefully conducted himself for some years prior to the sale in such a way as to be able to face the state at the end with the stark alternatives of allowing demolition or purchasing at a very high price. He helped his case forward with conservationist public opinion by a series of versions of the matter given to the press which by no means went into the full ins and outs of the situation. I became very conscious at this time of the restraints imposed by the decent custom we have whereby the state does not enter into a public discussion of the private financial affairs of individual citizens. That custom is a right one, so there is no more to be said about it here. The house was saved in the end, and the lessons we learned are, I hope, ticking away in the Whitehall machine, to issue in due course in legislative and administrative changes in this troublesome and complicated area of the relationship between estate duty and the preservation of our great houses. One of them, about break-up value, we put into the Preservation Policy Group Report.

Ever since 1913, when the system of state protection of historic buildings containing an element of compulsion was first introduced, churches in use as such have been exempt from preservation control, and have not received preservation grants. This was done at the instance of the Church itself; Archbishop Davidson made an important speech in the House of Lords on July 8 of that year which was taken as a request for exemption from state control.

A complicated system was introduced under the Pastoral Measure of 1968 which set up a Redundant Churches Fund (the first chairman being that doughty fighter Mr Ivor Bulmer Thomas) and allowed church and State to contribute the small sum of £200,000 each over a period of five years for the preservation of churches declared redundant by the former. But the time was coming, and everybody knew it, and it has now just about come, when fine old churches still in use are going to start falling down. Voluntary funds have done wonders, but can hardly meet the future. It is an enormous problem; there are 18,000 parish churches and 41 cathedrals in England; 11,000 of the former and all the latter are of architectural or historical interest. There are also several hundred more modest but still interesting nonconformist and Roman Catholic buildings, also exempt from preservation control and also debarred from grants.

The Places of Worship Commission of the Church Assembly, under the chairmanship of Professor Arthur Phillips, twice came to see me and raised the possibility of grants being made without the termination of the 'ecclesiastical exemption' from local and central government preservation control. I said there was no chance of grants without an end to the exemption and also that, even if the exemption was ended, there was no chance of grants on a meaningful scale in the immediate future, as long as present financial stringencies lasted. I took this line because I was convinced that the historic towns, and indeed listed buildings under state control generally, were more in need of whatever money was available than churches were. We were not losing fifty historic churches a year, which would be the same proportion as we were losing of listed lay buildings. But as soon as the Preservation Policy Group Report and the 3 million annual public expenditure (central and local together) on historic towns were in the bag, Roy Jenkins and I were agreed that churches in use might well be the next category for state aid. Half a million a year seemed a reasonable starting figure, and it could be spent on the advice of the Historic Buildings Council, perhaps with one or two specialist members added for the purpose. But that, of course, was only a month or so before we lost the Election.

There is a strong faction in the Church which wants every penny to go on pastoral work, and will firmly resist any expenditure on preserving old churches. If ever this faction is overridden by its opponents, the Church can come to the State and ask for the termination of the 1913 arrangement, just as it asked for it to be introduced. If and when it does, the Government of the day must take a decision. If the historic towns money remains cancelled, it will be hard to see how money for churches can be justified. But if it is ever reinstated, there is a

good case for the churches to benefit next. The right
course for the present Government is, therefore, to rein-
state in full the cancelled Exchequer grant for the
historic towns and at the same time to end the 'ecclesiastical exemption' if the Church wishes it, and begin
paying grants for churches in use. Jointly, these two
decisions might cost the Exchequer £2 million a year
to begin with, £1½ million on historic towns, and £½
million on churches, and the local authorities £1½ million a year.

That is an opinion about what the state ought to do.
But one may also have an opinion about what the Church
ought to do. Fine old churches are the accumulated piety
of our ancestors; they are lasting praise. It seems to me
hard to take the out and out pastoralist position, and say
that these churches may now be demolished, without
saying also that our ancestors were wrong to build Durham and Peterborough and Long Melford and St
Endelion. They were built in times of sin and poverty.
Do we have more sin and poverty than they did, that
no penny of ours shall go on preserving what they
built? And do the pastoralists never meet those agnostics,
perhaps a majority, to whom a fine church is the most
substantial of all witness to the faith?

A balance sheet of the four years' work is hard to draw
up. On the whole, though, it seems to have been favourable. When Labour came in, we found a public opinion
becoming yearly more and more certain that it wanted
to keep its architectural heritage, but we found within
the Ministry of Housing a very small, downtrodden and
sometimes quite cynical section responsible for the work.
I have mentioned how Crossman stopped the reductions
in staff, and began to increase it. After his departure I
managed (though only because of his initial impetus)
to get the corps of investigators doubled, from nine to
nineteen. They finished the first time round listing of
all the buildings in England in 1969. It had taken them

more than twenty years, and the number statutorily listed now stands at 119,000. They have already begun the second round listing, including this time Victorian buildings, a few of the most important buildings up to 1939, and buildings which, though not listable in themselves, contribute to an important group. Public opinion continues to increase in weight and certainty. The Civic Trust reckons the first local amenity society was founded in 1846, and by 1939 there was 101. In 1964 it had about 300 on its books. Now it has 760.

The cancellation by the new Conservative government of the General Conservation Schemes, and the £3 million annual public expenditure to make them possible, is the first setback in the development of public policy on preservation since it began in 1873. Periods of inertia, periods of insensitivity there have been, but, as the history told here shows, there has not before been an actual step backwards. This first step backwards is also a big one. It must be, and is being, roundly blamed by all that growing multitude who are aware of their surroundings. The press was virtually unanimous in calling for central government aid, and quite unanimous in ·condemning its cancellation.

But the various other measures we took, and especially Part V of the 1968 Town and Country Planning Act, have begun to show results. In 1966, as I said, we guessed that 400 listed buildings were lost. It was a guess, since no-one had bothered to find out for certain. In 1969 we were able for the first time, under the new provisions of the 1968 Act, to get a reliable figure. It had come down to 266, and I returned to Chester, as I had promised, in order to announce it. Chester had justified our earlier hopes; they, alone of all the towns in England, had actually introduced a twopenny rate for preservation. In January 1971 Lord Sandford, the present Parliamentary Secretary at the Department of the Environment responsible for preservation, announced that the figure for 1970 was 198. That continues a linear reduction. If the 1966 guess was right, it means we halved the rate of loss in four years, which is not bad. Indeed we rather more than halved it, since during those years the statutory list of buildings was increased from about 90,000 to about 120,000. So while the loss in 1966 was one in two hundred and twenty-five, the loss in 1970 was one in six hundred.

If the linear rate of loss continues to decrease at fifty a year, there will be no more listed buildings lost at all after 1974. But this is certainly too much to hope. Even stone decays, and wood and plaster decay quite quickly; Durham Cathedral itself will fall down or be rebuilt in facsimile sooner or later. If on the other hand the halving time of the rate of loss remains constant at four years, we shall be losing 100 a year in 1974, 50 a year in 1978, and 25 a year in 1982. Even that would be fairly satisfactory. But if the money is not forthcoming from a government whose scale of values does not allow them to understand its needfulness, nothing like this will be achieved, and the job of introducing a system for the preservation of our heritage which is worthy of our ancestors, of ourselves, and of our descendants, to say nothing of our tourist trade, will remain to be completed by another sort of Government.

This chapter has been an account of four years only in the developing history of preservation law and administration, and it has been an account of that as seen by only one of the protagonists. Everything was done with the blessing and backing of two successive ministers, Richard Crossman and Anthony Greenwood, and could not have been done without it. Nor could it has been done without the tireless work of the civil servants concerned. In one episode some of them, remaining nameless, appear above in an unfavourable light. I have related this piece of Whitehall in-fighting not because it was typical, it was far from that; but because I found it intensely interesting, and it seems it may be interesting to the general reader as well.

Our Permanent Secretary at the time, Sir Matthew Stevenson, though he had immense gifts of courage and foresight, was not a man who would by himself have given preservation a high priority in government activity. But when he saw that I was in earnest, and that Mr Greenwood backed me, he arranged for Mr Vivian Lipman to take over as the senior administrator to be exclusively concerned with these matters. Mr Lipman, an historian of Jewry, and a man with a wide knowledge and grounding of architectural history, bore with tigerish perseverance the burden of swinging the Whitehall machine in the new direction. With him worked Mr P. S. Waddington, a sensitive planner who pioneered the introduction of preservation values on the professional side of the Ministry. He it was who backed and protected Mr Roy Worskett, our professional adviser on townscape and how to handle it. Mr Worskett's firm judgment and wily tactics have saved more towns than will ever know it from fates worse than death. He did not always say very much and, when it was a town I did not know, I was often guided by Mr Worskett's eyebrows.

But what can be done by a government department is only what people in general want done, and there was during those years a wealth of eloquent and devoted interpreters of that. I have already praised Sir John Betjeman and Sir Nikolaus Pevsner. The ability of Lord Euston, now the Duke of Grafton, skilfully and unobtrusively to guide the work of an apparently limitless number of organisations, meant that he carried an immense public load. The ruthless enterprise of Mr Duncan Sandys in setting up the Civic Trust—I say ruthless because that is what he is when it comes to fund-raising—made possible a general raising of standards among all the hundreds of local amenity societies which are the grassroots of national preservation effort. And among the secretaries of the various national preservation bodies Mrs Jane Fawcett, of the Victorian Society, stood out as the most intransigent of the enemies of second-best solutions. She accorded no laurels, and therefore ensured there was no rest.

It was exhausting working with these people, but it was highly enjoyable.

III

Advice to amenity societies

In this chapter, I shall make some observations intended to be helpful to local amenity societies and to those meaning to set them up. First, I have to disclaim any wish to supersede or improve upon the excellent advice given in two Civic Trust pamphlets by Mr Arthur Percival, 'The Organisation of an Amenity Society' (1967) and 'Local Amenity Societies and Local Government' (1968). Where he writes of internal organisation and how to raise public interest, I shall write more of how to pick one's way through the law as it now stands.

But first, an admonition; a homily. It concerns local democracy. Local amenity societies are usually started by middle class people (though if they continue to have solely middle class membership that is probably a sign something is wrong). More, they are commonly started by middle class people whose education has been on the arts side, if one may include architecture in that. Now there is at the moment a phenomenon in this country so strange and so grave that it seems perhaps disproportionate to discourse about it in a short book on what is, after all, a topic of less than life and death importance. There is a full-fledged *trahison des clercs*. No self-respecting intellectual or aesthete would soil his hands with politics at all if he could help it, and certainly not with local politics. 'The Chamber was a low-roofed room, very dark, and very dirty, with some small rooms off it for clerks. Within this Pandemonium sat the town-council, omnipotent, corrupt, impenetrable. Nothing

108

was beyond its grasp; no variety of opinion disturbed its unanimity.' Lord Cockburn's famous description of the Edinburgh City Council in the 1790s raises an instant laugh, and an instant feeling of self-justification.[1] Things haven't changed much after all, have they? Local councillors are, after all, a shortsighted and mercenary class of persons, mostly shopkeepers. Come to that, members of parliament are mostly clever people fallen prey to some sort of neurotic compulsion to partisanship; it is obviously a decay of talent if it is turned to scoring cheap party points in the middle of the night. So let us return to higher matters; literature, music, the arts, *Kunstgeschichte*, love and science.

Such an attitude is, in the strict and original sense of the word, *idiotic*. The inventors of democracy, if one may call the ancient Greeks that, knew well enough that the one thing it could not survive, the one thing more dangerous to it than corruption or despotism, was an indifferent or contemptuous ignorance. This is what was meant by 'idiocy'; he who abstained from the practice of democracy (or indeed from a part in public affairs commensurate with his ability whatever the form of government might be) was an *idiotes*, a silly, private, selfish fellow. To be an 'idiot' in a tyranny was to prolong it; to be an 'idiot' in a democracy was to facilitate the advent of a tyrant.

All this is as true of modern Europe as it was of ancient Greece; if people in a democracy do not practice democracy, it will not last. Democracy is its own lifeblood, and Britain at the moment is anaemic.

In Britain at the moment, such 'idiocy' is rampant. All sane and generous people who have travelled to countries where there is tyranny or where there is a democracy far gone towards it, know that to live in such a country is a very miserable thing. Few of those who

<hr>

[1] Henry Cockburn *Memorials of his time*, Edinburgh, Black, 1861, p. 95.

lost or risked their lives in the Second World War did so for reasons other than to avoid the installation of a tyranny in this country, and few of those too young to have done either believe they were wrong. Churchill's adage 'Democracy is the worst form of government in the world except for all the others' is not only a chortle, it is also, like many things he said, a potential call to arms. The obligation to cherish and maintain the least bad is no less absolute than the obligation to cherish and maintain the best. It is the same.

Many people, though willing to die for democracy, do not know how it works and are sure that, even if they did, they themselves would be much above the task of working it. It works in a very complicated way. Many general human laws govern it, and it makes many specific laws of its own, to govern humans. The laws within each of these two classes are multifariously related, and the relation between the two classes is the highest study there is. Those who understand these two sorts of laws are wise: it could be held they are the wisest people in our community. Those who devote their lives to making the latter sort are good; it could be held they are the best people in our community. It is necessary to hammer a little on this point; if we do not believe it is wisdom which gets people elected to Parliament and to local councils, and if we do not believe it is virtue which impels them to labour at making the laws to which we owe our lives, we are either committed against democracy or, which is more likely, we are 'idiots', in that original sense. (In the former case we are bound, of course, to say what we are committed to. If we fail to say this we qualify for the higher grade of 'idiocy'; we are active 'idiots', or anarchists, instead of the more common passive sort.)

Let us consider now our local councillor. Is he corrupt? Is he stupid? He may be; some are. Perhaps indeed the level of corruption and stupidity is especially high among local councillors. It is impossible to measure such levels, but having had a good look at local councillors, at professionals, at businessmen, and at trade unionists, I incline to the view that local councillors are certainly no more than average corrupt and stupid, and probably less. But this does not matter; whatever the corruption and stupidity index, that is just human failure. It is some time since anybody held the human failings of priests to disprove the existence of God. I will return to the question of corruption later.

Let us assume for the moment that our local councillor is reasonably honest and intelligent, and come back to where we started. You are a member, perhaps the founder, of a local amenity society, and you have got to work out a relationship with this councillor and with others like him. You are almost sure to know a great deal more about the history of architecture, and likely to know a great deal more about history in general than he does. You may very well know more about planning, or traffic, or economics, or almost everything. But there is one thing that he knows more about than you, and that is politics, which is the relation between natural law and the transient laws man makes for himself. He knows a hundred unspoken things, things which he probably could not speak even if he wanted to, about the way people shake down together, about who will stand what, about what is fair to whom, *and you owe your peace and well-being to his knowledge.* Treat him with the respect that suggests. If your knowledge and intelligence are superior to his, as they may well be, you would have been elected more easily than he was. Therefore he has taken more trouble for the common good than you have.

I said we owe our peace and well-being to him. All this goes also for Members of Parliament in yet greater measure, since it is not only our peace and well-being which we owe to them, but our lives. The local councils were invented by Parliament, and Parliament was invented by you. You have a vote for both.

I personally, Wayland Young, second Lord Kennet, can write these things because I am one of those few people who, though not elected, has passed much of his active life among elected politicians doing the same work as them. Like everyone else, I hold a corrupt or thoughtless politician in contempt, and like everyone else, I rage and fume against politicians who, though honest and intelligent, I believe have mistaken the nature of man and society. But I cannot, because I have seen it done from close to, and have thought much about it, and have a little shared in the easier part of it, believe that the practice of democratic politics is less than the noblest and most useful calling professed among us. From this homily, whence we shall now descend to more workaday matters, it can only be deduced that you ought to stand for the Council. And so you ought.

The natural history of preservation, and indeed of the conservation and creation of amenity in general, seems in any place to fall into four phases. Phase I is before the foundation of the amenity society. The Council consists of those who have been elected to keep the rates down and the revenue up, to provide services which people feel are insufficient, or lacking, and generally to make the place known in the world. These are not unworthy aims, and the electors who wished them pursued are not unworthy people. This is the background which preservationists must accept gladly, and onto which they must graft their own equally worthy, but less familiar, work.

Phase II is when the amenity society is first formed, when the brigadiers and the poets, in uneasy alliance, descend upon the Town Hall and tell the Council they are a lot of Philistines.

Phase III is when a good working relation is developed between the Council and the Amenity Society. There is a flow of information both ways; the Council seeks the Society's advice: the Society offers help to the Council.

1 and 2 Beaufort Square, Bath—1945 and now. See page 131.

Barton Street, Bath: the back of the house in plate 2. See page 138.
4 The Hall, Gosport. See page 154.

Phase IV is when so many members of the Society are on the Council, and so many Councillors are automatically members of the Society, that one may wonder if the Society is any longer necessary. This phase has not yet been durably reached anywhere in England, and when it is, no doubt another and younger society will arise to dispute the fact, thus entering Phase II on its own account.

In what follows, then, I will assume that you are either in Phase II or Phase III, and, if the former, that you hope soon to be in the latter.

Here, then, is the house, street, square, quarter or village which you want to help preserve. It is presumably rather run down, or you would not be worrying about it. So there is no time to lose.

First, you must become familiar with the *Plan*. The 1947 Act laid on Local Planning Authorities (counties and county boroughs) the duty of surveying their areas and deciding what would be the best use for each part of the land in them. They were to do this within three years, and to repeat the process continuously so that every five years from then on they could submit to the Minister a *Development Plan*. Few indeed are the Planning Authorities who have actually kept to that rhythm, but all have submitted one or more development plans to the Minister since 1950.

When the Minister (now the Secretary of State for the Environment) gets the Plan, he assesses the amount of opposition there is to the proposals in it and, if there is enough to justify it, he holds a *Development Plan Enquiry*, at which those with something to say go along and say it. The Inspector who has taken the Enquiry then writes his report to the Secretary of State, and the Secretary of State *approves*, or *modifies*, or *rejects* the draft development plan. If he wishes to *modify* it, he must publish his proposals in draft form, because there may be objections to them to. If there are, there will probably have to be a public enquiry into the *Draft*

Modifications to the Development Plan, after which the Secretary of State will make his final decision.

All this is conveniently known as the *planning cycle;* the cycle being survey, submission of draft plan, enquiry into draft plan, publication of Secretary of State's proposed modifications, enquiry into modifications; confirmation of plan; and then once more; survey, submission, etc. The 1947 Act intended the cycle to take five years.

The 1968 Planning Act changed this cycle in the following way. It said that planning authorities were no longer to make all the rather detailed *development plans* which they had made before, but three separate classes of plans. The first are to be *structure plans,* which will differ from development plans in being more general and expressed more in words than in maps. These will be subject to the planning cycle as before; which may now be called the *structure plan cycle.*

Then the planning authorities are also to make *local plans,* which they will do by themselves, without ministerial intervention or confirmation. The *local plan cycle* will therefore by much shorter, consisting of local survey, publication of draft local plan, public discussion thereof, publication of modifications arising out of public discussion, further public discussion if need be, and lastly adoption by the Planning Authority. Though the *local plan* cycle lasts for a shorter time than the *structure plan cycle,* it need not be happening all the time.

The third new kind of plan is called the *action area plan.* This is really detailed and immediate; it is to be adopted in the same way as the local plan, the cycle being very short and, naturally, not needing to be recommenced for some time after the implementation of the plan. Action area plans need only be made if anybody, whether the Council itself or a private developer, or both together, is undertaking a phase of radical transformation of some spot. There should always be a structure plan in force for the whole of a Planning

Authority's area, there should be local plans covering much of it, but there need only be action area plans where there is action.

The layers under the new system are thus:

1 *Structure plan*: large-scale, general and long-term, needing Ministerial approval

2 *Local plan*: medium scale, medium detailed, medium term, and needing no ministerial approval

3 *Action area plan*: small-scale, detailed and immediate, needing no ministerial approval

When the 1968 Planning Act came into force, many planning authorities were at a point on the old *development plan cycle* where to have gone over at once to the new system would have been to waste work. Indeed it is obvious there is only one point of the cycle where it makes sense to go over to the new system, and that is at the very beginning of it. When an old style *development plan* is confirmed by the Secretary of State, then it makes sense to commence the survey for the next round of strategic planning in such a way as to lead in due course to a new style *structure plan*. Or it may make sense to use the results of a survey already nearly or quite complete to make a new style *structure plan* instead of an old style *development plan*. It will not make sense to try and convert an old style *development plan* into a new style *structure plan* once it is first formulated.

Moreover, the Government did not, and I expect still does not, believe that all planning authorities were yet good enough to be cast loose on the new system with its much lesser degree of Whitehall control. The Labour Government's strategy was to turn them over one by one, over several years, relying on the formation of larger, all-purpose local authorities under the local government reform programme of 1970 to provide skills

and staff enough to make it safe later in those places
where it would not immediately have been so. What will
happen now that local government is to be reformed by
a Conservative Government on the old two-tier pattern,
and that planning is still to be largely left to the lower
tier, remains to be seen.

So; what is the status of the plan which applies to the
house, street, square, quarter or village in which you are
interested? Is it an old style (1962 Act) Plan? Or a new
style (1968 Act) Plan? In either case, where is it on the
cycle? In the latter case, which level of plan is it: structure, local, or action area? The Planning Officer will
tell you. It will be in one of three positions on the cycle,
and this is perhaps the most important question for you.
Either it is still under preliminary discussion, in which
case you will tell the planning officer of your interest in
seeing the thing preserved. Or, secondly, it is at a phase
of statutory consultation or enquiry, in which case you
will go along and give your view and your evidence
formally. Or, thirdly, it is hard and fast, fixed by the
Secretary of State or by the Council itself, according to
the type of plan it is. If it is hard and fast the way you
want it, that is the end of your first phase of work. If it
is hard and fast the way you don't want it, that is not
necessarily the end. It is open to Planning Authorities
to make *modifications* to their own plans. If those are
old style *development plans* or new style *structure plans,*
such modifications require the Secretary of State's
approval. If they are new-style *local plans* or *action area
plans,* they do not. It is also open to planning authorities
to give or withhold specific planning permissions in a
way which does not conform to the plan which is in
effect. If the giving or withholding of such permissions
constitutes in their opinion a *departure* from the plan,
they must have ministerial approval for it. If it does not,
they can go right ahead and do it. Mark that the question whether or not the non-conforming permisison or
refusal *constitutes* an outright departure from the plan

is decided by the Planning Authority, not the Secretary of State.

If a *modification* or *departure* is submitted to the Secretary of State, he will commonly hold a public enquiry into it, unless it is merely the rectification of some oversight in the original plan, or the removal of some anomaly, so that there is no public opposition to it.

So, if the plan is already hard and fast in the way you don't like, you can press the Council to modify it (in the case of the minor new-style plans) to submit departure proposals (in the case of new-style *structure plans*, or old-style *development plans*) or to give or withhold the planning permissions you are interested in, and deem them insufficient in effect to constitute a *departure*. Note that you cannot ask the Secretary of State to modify or reject a plan he has approved, or to tell a Planning Authority it is wrong in saying that permissions given or withheld do not constitute a departure. You can ask the Secretary of State to hold a public enquiry into a submission from the Council which is before him and which you do not like, and if you have yourself applied for planning permission in respect of any land, and it has been refused, you can appeal to him against its refusal by the Council.

All three of the new types of plan are likely to be of interest to amenity societies. It is the *structure plan* of a county, for instance, that decides which villages are to be encouraged to grow, which are to be allowed to grow under natural economic impulsion, which are to be discouraged from growing, and which are to be rigidly held down to their present size. Amenity societies usually have very strong views about this question. If you come apart on it, no matter; you will just have to fight the issues out with rival amenity societies before the Planning Authority itself. That's what it's there for. The structure plan in a city or big town will normally show roughly where the new roads are to go, which quarters are to be continued in their present form of use and which changed to another, as: industrial, shopping, offices, residential and so on. It will also show where new housing development is proposed on the outskirts.

Local plans will show exactly where new and widened roads are to be, where a new school or college is to be built, and so on. *Action area plans* will show house by house and fence by fence what is to be done.

At all stages, the Planning Authority is bound to tell you what is going on. I say: at all stages. There are extremists who hold that if a Planning Officer sketches something out on the back of an envelope during the lunch hour, he is guilty of clandestine tyranny if he has not published it in the evening paper. It is necessary for Planning Officers to have ideas, and to be allowed to work their ideas out to a certain extent before telling anyone else about them; this is because we have adopted the division of labour. Theoretically, every citizen and every group of citizens, could be presenting ideas for discussion all the time. But they don't, so the Planning Officer has to. If he has not told you about it before, it does not mean it is too late for you to affect it now, it may simply mean he was afraid you'd laugh at it if you saw it in the way it was last month.

The 1968 Planning Act, its schedules, and the regulations made under it, provide that you must have an opportunity of participating in the formulation of every plan, and of stating your view on every single planning application. The law is complex and in a way rather beautiful in its complexity. If you enjoy that sort of thing, it is well worth reading. If not, you are on perfectly safe ground in asserting to the Planning Officer that any planning decision of any sort, which was taken without your having been given an opportunity of saying what you think about it, has been improperly taken. I say 'given an opportunity': if you are given it and do not take it, that is your look-out. The Planning Officer does not have the staff to knock on your door with a copy of each day's workload for your gentlemanly perusal.

You must read the local paper, you must walk around the place and see the notices, you must call at the Town Hall and ask to see the Register.

As soon as you get into Phase III, all this will be second nature, both to you and to the Planning Department. But let us assume you are still in Phase II; what is the best manner to adopt? Mr Percival, in his Civic Trust pamphlets, has excellent advice on this, and his 'how not to do it' exchange of letters between the Secretary of the Fossilby Society and the Clerk of the Fossilby Urban District Council has become a classic in planning and amenity circles. It is as he says; get the facts right, be consistent, be courteous.

The homily with which I opened this chapter was not intended to make you think you should bow and scrape before the Council and all its officers, or tremble at their lightest word. For one thing, it is the Councillor who is automatically entitled to a certain kind of respect, not necessarily the officers. There is no presumption that they are any wiser or better than you; they are people doing a paid job and must earn your respect as any others would. The Councillor himself, of course, may be set on what you consider a wrong course, in which case you will no doubt oppose him in it, though not necessarily in other things. There is a world of difference between opposition, even fierce opposition, to a given policy or proposal, and ignorant contempt for the office, the man who holds it, and the way he got it.

It is common for beginners in an amenity society to worry about 'alienating the Council'. This is not possible; the Council is yours, inalienably. Of course you may alienate individual councillors, or the Planning Officer or the Clerk. Indeed if you start off with a bang on a particular issue, as you probably will, you are almost bound to alienate someone or other, who has been working devotedly for years on the proposal you have only just heard of, and which you don't like. But you cannot alienate the Council as such. It is there to

take account of everybody's point of view, and you are
advancing a point of view which is just as valid as
anyone else's. It may decide against you in the end,
but that will be because it thinks the other view is on
the whole more in the public interest; it will not be
because it doesn't like your face. So there is nothing to
be gained by timidity or subservience. Be firm but not
hectoring, courteous but not diffident, brief but not curt,
and accurate but not niggling. The planners are quite
likely to be busier than you, and even if they are not
it is always a pleasant courtesy to treat people as if
they are.

As to what you might actually seek to do about the
run-down house, street, square or quarter you are interested in; it clarifies the mind to think in terms of the
three approaches which I earlier described as the Aubrey,
the Stukeley and the Lubbock—the Aubrey, gaining
direct control of the building; the Stukeley, making the
owner ashamed of wanting to pull it down; the Lubbock,
having and using laws saying it may not be pulled
down. By far the best will be if you can own it; prefer
the straight Aubrey. If you can raise the money and
buy, you have two points in hand; you have saved that
particular building, and you have shown others that such
things can be done. There are all sorts of grants to help
you, some of which I have already mentioned. The
Council will tell you about them, but remember to make
sure you have got a note of every single one that could
come in. Talk to the Housing Department as well as the
Planning Department.

Next best is to shame the present owner into preserving it. The owner may be the Council itself; local councils have come, one way and another, to possess an
amazing amount of our towns. Often they hardly realise
it themselves. In that case, have recourse to the Stukeley,
and take it for granted that the owner, whoever he is,
would never sacrifice so fine a thing 'for the little dirty
profit'. Even if the owner is a big developer, do not

despair. As the tide sets more strongly everywhere in favour of conservation, so more and more of the big developers can be persuaded to go some distance with it for the sake of their image. If it is a single fine building, or a small row, which interests you, standing among gubbins that could well go, you may be able to persuade a developer to incorporate it in his overall plans, renovating and keeping it among new buildings designed to harmonise with it. It will help if you display on the one hand a knowledge of preservation law, and a willingness to urge its use upon the Council, and on the other an understanding of what the developer is trying to do. It may, before you come along, be aesthetically disastrous, and you will try to make it better. It is probably not socially disastrous, and you will not help your case by saying it is. (Unless of course it *is*: but think this out very carefully.)

That is the Stukeley. There is also the Aubrey-Stukeley; this is half in half, and consists of raising half the money needed to buy and preserve. Having Aubreyed thus far, you Stukeley the other party into finding the rest of the money, and set up a joint ownership and management system as best suits the case. Alternatively again you can make over the money you have raised, being half the preservation price to the owner on condition that he does the rest. The York Civic Trust are past masters of the Aubrey-Stukeley.

In trying either the Aubrey or the Stukeley, you must be prepared to be left with a fine old building or street on your hands, and must therefore be ready with plans for what to do with it. This is a swiftly developing science, and it would be rash of me to say anything here, which may be put out of date by changing economic factors in a few years. At the moment, conversion to student lodgings is easily the front runner. But you may be in a place with no students. Flats in general are a good bet just now, but for that you also have to get the traffic out of the street, which doubles or trebles the work to be done. (Students put up with traffic; partly because they are only there for a short time, and partly because there is usually only one thing at a time they won't put up with, and traffic isn't it.) As to uses, it is best to consult the Civic Trust.

But you cannot limit your efforts to the property you can afford to buy, and such is the world that you will often fail to shame the present owner into doing what he should. Then you must fall back on the Lubbock, and strengthen the hand of the Council in every way you can, so that it uses the very comprehensive battery of powers it now has.

First you must find out whether the house in question is on the Statutory List. If it is not, and if you are convinced that it should be, and should be preserved, you must try to persuade the Council to place a *building preservation notice* on it. This will protect it for six months, and make one of the Minister's investigators come and have a look at it, within six months, to see if he thinks it should be statutorily listed. You should give the investigator any information you have about its history (or give it to the Council for him), but should not attempt to sway his opinion. When he has seen the investigator's report, the Secretary of State will decide whether to list it.

But you are far more likely to find the building is already listed and in that case, or if the Minister lists it as a result of the Council's intervention, the owner cannot demolish or alter it without a form of permission from the local planning authority called a *listed building consent.*[1] You must seek by all means to induce the Local Planning Authority to refuse that consent since, once they have given it, there is very little more that anyone can do. If you think they are going to give it, you can (and, provided you are confident of your case you should) ask the Secretary of State to call the matter in for his

[1]See p. 77.

own decision. And, if the local Authority has given consent, you can in fact ask the Secretary of State to revoke it over their heads; but if he does this he will lay on your local rates the full cost of the development value which the developer is done out of by his action. So he is unlikely to do that.

In seeking to persuade the Planning Authority to refuse consent, you should strongly make the point that, if they allow it, this is in fact the end of the matter; whereas if they refuse it, it is not the end: their refusal will probably lead to the Minister holding a public enquiry at which both sides will be able to argue the case. It is not therefore 'yes' or 'no' to demolition; it is 'yes', or 'let's discuss it'.

If, in spite of your efforts, the Council grants listed building consent, there is, as I said, nothing more you do under the law. But it is conceivably worth trying a posthumous Stukeley and saying to the developer: 'Although you have a perfect right to demolish this, we know that you and you alone are such wonderful people that you will not do it.' I never heard of this working.

If on the other hand the Council refuse consent, whether because they accept your arguments or for any other reason, two things can happen. Either the owner will accept defeat, or he will appeal. If he accepts defeat, he will want either to sell the building or to renovate it himself. In either case he may be glad of your help; in the first case you may want to buy it or help him find a purchaser; in the latter he may want your advice on how to renovate and what use to put the renovated building to. So if there is no appeal, (ask his lawyer if he intends to appeal) make a point of getting in touch with the owner and offering your help.

If on the other hand the owner appeals against refusal of listed building consent, the first thing the Secretary of State must do is decide whether the appeal shall be considered 'on written representations', or by means of

a public local enquiry. The former means that the
appellant, the Council who have refused him permission,
and you, and anybody else who is interested, simply
write to the Secretary of State and say what you think,
and then he makes up his mind. The public local
enquiry involves a day or more of semi-formal proceedings before an Inspector. You should make up your
mind which you want. Written representations are
cheaper and easier for all concerned and are considered
just as carefully as the Inspector's report after a public
enquiry. So there is no harm in choosing that for minor
cases. But for a major case a public local enquiry is
obviously better, if only because of the greater opportunity it gives you to hit the local press. Formerly Ministers fairly often decided to settle appeals on written
representations whether or not there was a demand for
public local enquiry. This hardly ever happens nowadays, and if you want an enquiry you are increasingly
likely to get one.

If you do, you should give some thought to the manner
in which you present your evidence. If there are many
people—perhaps hundreds or even thousands who all
think the same as you—you will not endear yourself
to the Inspector or to anyone else if you encourage them
all to come along and say so. Get them all to sign a
single petition. If on the other hand, there are a number
of people, perhaps five or eight, each of whom has a
different point to make, but all tending to the conclusion that the building, street, or village should be saved,
it is well worth while making sure that each of them
comes and speaks.

Then there is the Council itself. Since the enquiry is
into an appeal against the local authority's refusal of
consent, they are by definition on the same side as you.
You should, if the Council like it that way, concert your
evidence with theirs. There may be some specialist
points they will be glad to leave to you, and others,
particularly those which must rest on expensive statis-

tical work, for instance traffic surveys, which are best presented by the Council. Your part is to make sure the Council do not overlook their significance.

Contrary to a common belief there is no general need to be represented by a barrister or a solicitor: it may be a waste of your hard-gotten money. The Secretary of State's Inspector may well strike you as a tactiturn and inscrutable individual. But it is his life's work to know how to give as much weight to a case put in a muddled or inconclusive way as to one put with periclean clarity. Nor should you be afraid of standing up to examination from counsel for the appellants: if the Inspector allows them to examine you at all, and he may not, he will take great care that you are not brow-beaten. It is likely, though, at large enquiries and on occasions when the other side employ counsel, perhaps into structure plans or into local plans covering a whole area of a city, if you are well in funds, that you may think it rational to spend the money on having a trained advocate to follow the matter through the many days of sittings. In general you should not find a public local enquiry very like a court. Inspectors try not to look enthroned or numinous, and if a courtroom atmosphere develops, that is against the intention of the Government which devised the 1968 Act and of the Parliament which passed it, and it would not be out of place to say so.

After the enquiry is closed there is nothing more you can do. Indeed, if you write to the Secretary of State you will either be repeating what you said at the enquiry, in which case the Inspector will already have told him about it, or you will be saying something new, in which case he will not be allowed to take it into account, because the other side will not have had the opportunity of commenting on it. If something new has happened since the end of the enquiry and if it is really important, then you should write to the Secretary of State telling him about it and asking him to re-open the enquiry so that it can be laid before the Inspector and the other side can say what it thinks about the new evidence. Send a copy of your letter to the Council.

I have been quite often asked by amenity societies: 'One of our members knows the Secretary of State (or one of the junior Ministers): is it in order for him to write personally?' The answer is yes, so long as he doesn't use his acquaintance or intimacy to seek to influence the Secretary of State's decision. About thirteen thousand planning appeals are received in the Department each year, and it may be that the Secretary of State or one of his junior Ministers will personally see three or four hundred of them. If he gets a letter from an old friend asking him to look at a particular case which is before him, he may well like to do so, not because the case will thereby be decided otherwise than it would have been, but because he may be personally interested to see what his old friend is up to these days.

It may be that at an early stage in all this proceeding, an amenity society may find its local Council reluctant to refuse listed building consent or serve a building preservation notice for fear that it may be forced at the end of the day to buy the building concerned. You should then point out with all the force at your command that this cannot happen unless the owner of the building is deprived of the beneficial use of it, and that any building with a watertight roof and a front door that opens has a beneficial use of some sort, and that if it is not beneficial to the present owner he can sell it to someone to whom it will be beneficial, and that if it is so far gone that the roof leaks and the front door will not open the Council should long ago have used their powers to repair it, and that this fact is in any case evidence that the owner is deliberately allowing the building to decay with the intention of securing development value on the site. If this last is so, the Council is entitled to apply to the Minister for a *minimum compensation direction*[1] and, the worse the condi-

[1] See p. 84.

tion of the building, the less it will cost them if they have to buy it. All these arguments of course tend to push the Council into expenditure, whether for repair or purchase; and it is obvious that if you can help them with the repair bill or the purchase bill, or above all with a use for the building after they have purchased it, they will be the more inclined to listen to what you say.

In seeking to preserve fine old buildings, streets and squares, one often comes upon cases where the structure is so far gone, not necessarily through neglect but sometimes simply through well-used age, that the question of demolition and reconstruction in facsimile is bound to arise. The choice you make about this will be your own and will vary from place to place. But one thing you should beware of, and that is the *façade trick*. This goes as follows. A developer, typically a hotel chain, will demonstrate to everybody's satisfaction that a given old building can no longer be used, is not capable of renovation without gutting, is an obstacle to the proper development of the tourist trade, etc., etc. The Council, perhaps with the agreement of the local amenity society will, after tearing its hair for a bit, give the developer consent to demolish everything except the façade, and to erect a new building behind it. The developer will proceed to demolish what he is allowed to demolish and, having put up some plausible looking baulks and scaffolding round the façade, will, surprise surprise, discover that the latter is unsafe and must be demolished as well. This trick is now so widely practised that an amenity society should use all its powers of persuasion to prevent the local authority allowing any developer, except one with a well-known and faultless record for preservation, to re-develop behind an old façade. It should, on the contrary, urge the local authority to do the job itself, as it may, acting as the developer's agent and charging him for it. If the developer's intentions are honourable he will not object to this arrangement.

Quis, on the other hand, *custodiet ipsos custodes*? The Council's own intentions may not be honourable, and if they are not it will be no advantage to see to it that the façade trick is done by them for the developer instead of by him direct. This brings us to the whole question of the retrograde or corrupt Council. All that has gone before has tended to the conclusion that you should respect your individual Councillors as elected persons, and should as soon as possible achieve a good working relation with the Council, helping them and being helped by them to return. There are some local authority areas where there is no amenity society yet. There are many where the amenity society is in what I call Phase II: that is, in the process of achieving a useful relationship with the Council. There are some where no proper relationship has been achieved and a condition of apparently permanent guerrilla warfare continues, and where that is clearly the amenity society's fault. There are some where there is a guerrilla situation and it is hard to tell whether it is the society's fault or the Council's. But there are also a few where there is a guerrilla situation and it is clearly the Council's fault.

You should be slow to decide that you are in such a situation. If you have been seeking to establish a proper relationship with the Council and have got nowhere within a year, it would be as well to ask the Civic Trust and neighbouring societies whether you are setting about it the right way. If they say you are and you have still got nowhere within two years, then you will be forced to recognise that you are in that fortunately unusual situation: you have a retrograde or corrupt council. You will probably by then know which it is.

If it is retrograde, you will naturally wish to enlighten it, and the way to do this will be via public opinion. Interest the local press. If you can't interest them, it is probably a sign that they, as well as the Council, are corrupt, and you were wrong in supposing it was only retrogression. As regards the Council's own buildings

5 and 6 Gosport in the 1950s. Everything shown in these two has gone, including the trees and the gravestones. See page 154.

7 and 8 Where the Enfield Road would have gone. See page 163.

you should also remember that every power described above which the Council has over the operations of private owners and developers, the Secretary of State has over the Council. They must have his consent to demolish or alter their own listed buildings. If they do not look after them properly the Secretary of State can serve a repair notice on the Council, and at the end of the day it can acquire them from the Council with minimum compensation. It may well be worth while pointing all this out to the local press, radio and television.

Tell your MP about it. If all is going well between you and the Council, he will no doubt be interested to know of it, but there will be no need for him to do anything in Parliament. If on the other hand your Council is a notorious scandal in this, as in other respects, he will be glad to have an opportunity either of trying to reform them, or failing that, of blasting off at Westminster about it.

Corruption is a much more difficult and frustrating matter. No Councillor may vote on a question in which he has an interest, or speak on such a question without declaring his interest. But it is human nature to wish to be nice to one's colleagues, even when they have declared an interest and left the room. This is why it is so unfortunate that our laws about who may be a councillor and who may not are so lopsided. A fitter at the corporation bus depot may not be a councillor because he is a council employee and might therefore use his position to favour himself. A property developer who owns half the town, and to whom a planning permission given by the Council may be worth half a million, is not a council employee and so there is no danger of his using his position to favour himself, and he may be a Councillor. There are one or two county boroughs and counties in England at present where property interests and building interests are very much in the ascendant. You, as an amenity society, are just as likely to be able to get to the bottom of the matter as anybody else, and you ought to try. Cultivate the company of retired policemen, and get a good lawyer. It is no use writing to the Secretary of State or to anyone else saying you think the Council are corrupt, or a given councillor is. There's nothing he can do without evidence. If you are sure, give your evidence to the police. If they do nothing, then write to the Home Secretary. Every year now there are one or two cases of councillors brought to trial for corruption in planning matters.

But in almost all cases your energies will be best devoted to achieving a satisfactory and durable Phase III situation, and proceeeding smoothly from Stukeley to Aubrey and back again. In the next and final section, I give some case histories of how this has been done and in narrating them, I use the method of direct quotation from documents and press accounts wherever possible. These documents are very detailed, and may sometimes appear trivial. But the day to day business of preservation does in fact consist mainly of details. I have found in compiling these histories, and I hope the reader will find in reading them, that particular fascination which always attends a close study of the real; who did what next? And how; *precisely* how? Loose ends abound; initiatives end in nothing. But that is how life is, and these stories do show how a purpose can be achieved through a mass of detailed and time-consuming work.

IV

Case histories

BEAUFORT SQUARE, BATH

Beaufort Square in Bath was built in about 1730. The architect was John Strahan; his more famous contemporary, John Wood the Elder, conceded that 'the buildings have a sort of regularity to commend them, though the design is somewhat piratical.' They do not now remind us of John Wood himself, as he feared they might, but more of the miniature unities one finds in French towns of that date. The whole feeling is enclosed and ornamental; not sweeping and windy like John Wood. One side of the square consists of the Theatre Royal of 1805, the other three sides, at the end of the Second World War, were fairly much as Strahan had built them, though the unity had been infringed here and there.

The best remaining house was No. 5; it's neighbours, Nos. 3 and 4, had been replaced in the early nineteenth century by indeterminate but not unpleasing gubbins (Plate 1) and this gubbins had been condemned and demolished by the Council around 1956. The opportunity for minor road widening was taken, but the site thereupon lapsed into a car park while the Council explored the possibilities of re-development. Everything proposed at first appeared uneconomic, so when it was announced in 1961 that an economic solution had at last been found, there were official sighs of relief. This solution was to lease the site to a local developer. But the

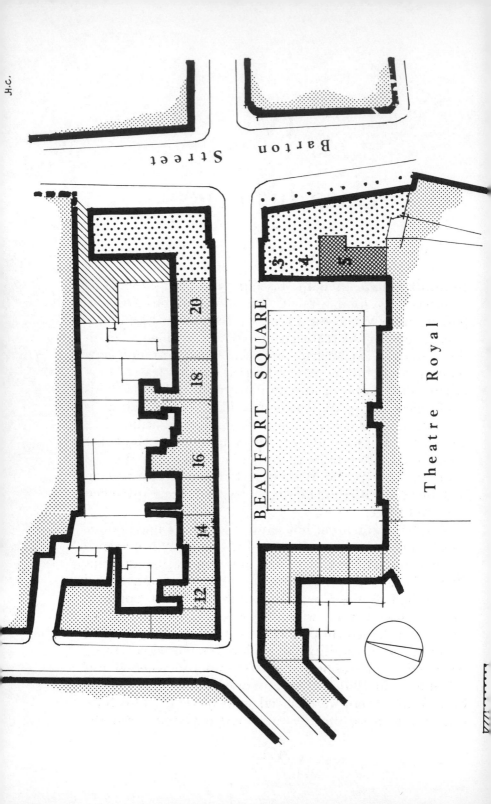

H.C.

Barton Street

BEAUFORT SQUARE

Theatre Royal

12   14   16   18   20

3   4   5

relief was shortlived: the developer made it a condition that the whole East end of the square should be cleared of the existing buildings.

The situation can be studied on the plan opposite. The East side of Beaufort Square backs on Barton Street, leading to Queen Square and already becoming an important North-South distributor on the West of the central core. The threatened house in Beaufort Square was the best one left, and was a Listed Building Grade II. Nor surprisingly, the proposal to demolish it, which would put paid for ever to any hopes of restoring the whole square, provoked a sharp reaction from the Bath Preservation Trust.

This Society, formed around 1910 to combat a specific threat, had been revived in 1929 as 'The Old Bath Preservation Society', known as 'the Old Preservers', and at one time, chaired by the then Mayor, had reached a membership of 1,000. Its present name and status dates from 1934 when drastic changes to Milsom Street were successfully resisted. The Chairman in 1961 was a founder Trustee, an ex-Councillor and a co-opted member of the Planning Committee. So the Trustees had naturally heard of the Council's perplexities over the Beaufort Square site.

The houses on the North side of the square, that is the bulk of the houses in it, were owned by the Bath Municipal Charities. Accordingly, in February 1960 the Bath Preservation Trust wrote to the Clerk of the Municipal Charities in part as follows:

My Trustees feel that as we understand the Municipal Trustees own the bulk of the remaining property in Beaufort Square they are vitally affected by any redevelopment scheme . . . I am instructed therefore to approach you with a view to suggesting that the Corporation should be asked to agree . . . to closing the vehicular access to Beaufort Square and substituting an archway providing for pedestrian access only. It is suggested that this course would materially enhance the value of the remaining properties in Beaufort

Square. Provision for access, e.g. by the fire engine, could be made at the far end of Beaufort Square, a removable post being set in the roadway.

The Municipal Charities replied as follows:

The Trustees have asked me to write and say that they appreciate the interest which your Trust takes in these properties, but they do not themselves consider that your proposals are for the benefit of their properties and they do not wish to take any action in the matter.

Having drawn a stony blank with the neighbouring property owners, the Preservation Trust then turned to the local press and wrote on the 11 November 1960 to the *Bath and Wilts Chronicle and Herald*:

It is greatly to be hoped that the Trustees (that is the Bath Preservation Trust) appeal for a comprehensive plan may now be adopted by the Planning Committee (of the Council) whether by promoting a competition for a suitable design amongst local architects or by the more usual course of instructing one architect to undertake the work. With imaginative treatment, Beaufort Square might again become a little oasis of peace and charm only a few minutes' walk from the busy centre of the city.

General interest in Beaufort Square now began to stir.

Councillor Hornblower to Councillor Mrs Maw (a Trustee of the Bath Preservation Trust) *30 October 1961:*

I recently contacted the City Engineer on the bad state of the footpath in Beaufort Square. He has informed me that the Bath Preservation Trust are hoping that this street can be preserved in natural pennant paving, and that if this proposal receives Council support the prohibitive cost would mean that special provision would have to be made in the Annual Estimates and that there would probably be considerable delay before the work could be carried out.

Bath Preservation Trust to Councillor Hornblower, 6 November 1961:

I would suggest that the City Engineer has misled you somewhat in regard to the prohibitive cost of preserving the pennant stone paving in the Square. It would indeed be prohibitive if new stone had to be bought, but there is an adequate stock of pennant stones held by the Council which have been removed from other pennants in the city.

Bath Preservation Trust to the Georgian Group, London 10 November:

The Corporation's present intention is to lease the whole site to a Bath builder on a Ninety-nine year lease of £100 p.a. with permission to demolish No. 5, subject of course to the permission of the Minister of Housing as it is a listed house. It is proposed to close the end of the Square by the new building, but to give access to vehicles to the Square by means of an archway. This part of the plan was originally suggested by our Trust but we hoped to see a new building which incorporated No. 5 and was in complete harmony with it.

The more distant photograph is intended to give an impression of the atmosphere of the Square. Most of the houses on the left are the property of Bath Municipal Charities.

The Georgian Group in London to the Bath Preservation Trust, 17 November:

The Group would fully support your Trust's efforts in seeking the preservation of this fine house. May we keep the photographs in the meantime?

Bath Preservation Trust to 'Peterborough', Daily Telegraph, 8 December 1961:

I understand that Lord Methuen is writing to you about the proposal by Bath City Corporation to demolish No. 5 Beaufort Square. It occurs to me that you may like to have a copy of the enclosed notes about the house which I sent to the Georgian Group. Lord Methuen tells me that he is sending you a copy of the Christmas card issued by the Trust this year. (The Christmas card was a sketch of the house in question.) 'The Trust would have no objection to the design being reproduced in your paper.

On December 14 the *Bath Evening Chronicle* published a letter from Lord Methuen suggesting that the existing square should be completed in the existing style 'with modern interiors at the back'. This was in fact the solution finally achieved.

Council for British Archaeology to the Bath City Council, 19 December:

'The Council has noted with concern a reference in "The Daily Telegraph" . . . The building as you know forms an integral part of one of the best Georgian sections in Bath and every effort should be made to retain it. On a purely commercial or material level it might be pointed out to the local authorities that the retention of the Georgian features in the city is of value since they form one of the main tourist attractions. American visitors to this country. . .

Bath Preservation Trust to the Editors of the Daily Express, *Press Association,* Bath Evening Post and Evening World, Bath and Wilts Chronicle, The Times, Daily Telegraph, Daily Mirror, Daily Mail, Guardian, Western Daily Press, Daily Herald, *2 January 1962:*

In recent weeks considerable feeling has been aroused both in and outside Bath by the announcement that the Corporation are prepared to countenance the demolishment of No. 5 Beaufort Square to make way for a block of flats. This matter has been considered by the . . . Bath Preservation Trust who think that the site is one which cannot be developed on a purely economic basis and they are prepared to sponsor a fund for the building of a suitable house to complete the Square. In view of the interest shown in Bath by various newspapers, it is proposed to hold a press conference to discuss the matter . . . The office is immediately above Messrs Shutters' shop. You are accordingly invited to send a representative.

Bath Preservation Trust to the Town Clerk of Bath, 4 January:

I sent out invitations to the press for a conference at this office on Monday next, the 8th January. On receipt of this letter the "Bath Chronicle" Editor, unable to contact me owing to my being in London yesterday, proceeded to print the story in their edition last night.

I greatly regret that this course should have been adopted by a local paper before I had advised you of the proposal and I now write to offer you my most sincere apologies for this discourtesy, which I would not have had happen for anything in the world. . . . If you wished to send a representative he would be welcome. His presence would not of course be taken as committing the Corporation in any way.

Town Clerk of Bath to Bath Preservation Trust, 5 January:

Thank you for your letter. . . I quite understand the position. I am endeavouring to arrange for the Chairman of the Planning Committee and the City Planning Officer to attend your meeting.

On January 8 the press conference took place and was attended by seven representatives of the Bath Preservation Trust, one from the City Council, and reporters from the *Daily Telegraph, Guardian, Bath Chronicle* and the *Bristol Evening Post* and *Evening World*. It resulted in features in *The Times* and *Guardian* and a leader in the *Bath Chronicle*.

Ministry of Housing and Local Government to Bath Preservation Trust, 25 January:

We were consulted informally in October last by the Bath Corporation. We replied that . . . No 5 is one of the best houses in the Square and its wide façade . . . was important to the character of the Square. Ideally we would prefer this house to be retained intact, but if this would unduly interfere with the proposed redevelopment we would regard the incorporation of the façade only as acceptable. It was assumed that the elevation of the new development looking inwards to the Square would be residential in character and in keeping with No 5 . . . as regards height and fenestration.

The original vision of the Preservation Trust, namely a building which should take its style from Beaufort Square and spill over into Barton Street echoing the small rhythms of the eighteenth century all the way, a sort of miniature Grand Trianon, now had to be compared with the alternative vision, put forward as such by Lord Methuen and arising automatically from a consideration of the law in the Ministry of Housing and Local Government: namely a building facing Barton Street which would simply have a false eighteenth century back on to Beaufort Square.

At the press conference, and in the letter they sent to the *Bath and Wilts Chronicle* the next day, the Preservation Trust estimated that

It would be a comparatively simple matter to build a companion house to the Christmas card house and so complete the east side of the Square once more, but it could not be represented as a business proposition. Letters of support for the campaign to save No. 5 have stressed the fact that Georgian Bath belongs to Europe and not to Bath alone. Is there in fact a sufficient weight of opinion to produce the money needed to replace No. 4 Beaufort Square and provide adequate treatment of the Barton Street frontage? A sum in excess of £10,000 might be required . . . Promises of financial support for this project should be sent to . . . All those informing the Trust of their concern about this matter will then be advised whether the support warrants proceeding with the preparation of a definite plan, or whether this delightful relic of eighteenth century domestic architecture must be allowed to be swept away by the bulldozers of economic necessity.

The letter was sent also to the *Spectator* and *Time and Tide*.

Bath Preservation Trust to Mr S. E. Vancouver:

In today's edition of the "Bath Evening Chronicle" there is an interesting account of your business career. . . . In view of your early connection with Beaufort Square I am writing to ask whether you will consider helping us in the appeal which was issued earlier this month. . . .

Town Clerk of Bath to Bath Preservation Trust, 2 February 1962:

5 Beaufort Square

I write to inform you that the Planning Committee have appointed the following of their number . . . to meet representatives of the Bath Preservation Trust for the purpose of ascertaining in detail the views of the Trust in respect of property at present owned by the Corporation. . . .

Bath Preservation Trust to the Town Clerk of Bath, 6 February:

The Trustees are happy to accept this invitation. . . . In regard to time we would endeavour to fit in with that most convenient to the Committee.

Surely, Sir, the property in question belongs to the citizens of Bath, whose views we represent.

Appeal Planning Ltd to Bath Preservation Trust, 5 February:

Our firm deals with appeals of all kinds. At present we are running one for —, another for —, and —, as well as numerous consultancies. I myself was born in Bath. We would be very interested in helping you towards raising money for your Trust. We have considerable experience in this form of business which has now become fairly specialised. Would it be convenient for you if I came down to see you?

Bath Preservation Trust to Appeal Planning Ltd:

I should be very pleased to discuss this problem with you at some mutually convenient date but I do not feel that it would be worth while your making a special trip to Bath for the purpose.

Appeal Planning Ltd to Bath Preservation Trust, 9 February:

As it happens I shall be staying in — for the week. We have an appeal running there at the moment for a large boys' school. The campaign director on the spot has been taken ill and I am going to stand in for him. Could I come down and call on you at Bath on Friday, 16th February? . . . It will be most interesting to discuss the Trust with you, especially as I am a Bathonian by ancestry.

The long prepared meeting between the Bath City Council and the Bath Preservation Trust took place at last on 23 February 1962. The Council told the Trust that the question of 5 Beaufort Square could not be considered in isolation. It must be considered as part of a comprehensive scheme which would involve the widening of the whole of Barton Street on its west side and the immediate redevelopment not only of that part of Barton Street which backed onto No 5 and the site of Nos 4 and 3 Beaufort Square, but also a distance about equal to that up Barton Street to the north. The Council was sympathetic to the aim of preservation, but it did not see how it could be done economically. It was prepared to do nothing for three months if the Preservation Trust would undertake during the period to produce a sketch plan of how the whole development might look, preservation included, and a statement of how much money it would itself be able to contribute in order to close the gap between outlay and return.

The Preservation Trust accepted the challenge.

Bath Preservation Trust to Appeal Planning Ltd, 8 March:

I am sorry that I have not written to you earlier . . . but events have been moving rather fast since I saw you. . . . It seems better to await developments before pressing our appeal further.

Appeal Planning Ltd to Bath Preservation Trust, 12 March:

I do hope that when you are in a position to go ahead with the appeal you will communicate with us again. We shall be delighted to be of service to you.

Public interest in the matter had now reached the level necessary to trigger an orthographic discussion: as all those familiar with preservation work know, this level is a useful indicator of widespread public concern. On March 27 Mr Herbert Fuller, a Trustee of the Bath Preservation Trust, sent to the Editor of the *Bath Evening Chronicle* and to the Bath Preservation Trust a comprehensive paper on whether Beaufort Square should be spelt Beaufort or Beauford. He listed twenty-three references with the spelling 't' between 1749 (John Wood) and 1945 (Lord Abercrombie) and sixteen with the spelling 'd' between 1735 and 1947. His conclusion was: 'From Wood's description there can be no doubt that these Buildings (later called Square) were named Beaufort after the Duke of Beaufort (of 1711). . . The official *A Plan for Bath*, 1945, acknowledges Beaufort as correct. Surely in all future reference to this Square Beauford should be dropped and Beaufort used, and the Bath Street Directory amended accordingly.'

Meanwhile the Preservation Trust had commissioned Mr Ernest Tew, FRIBA, to make the sketch plan that the City Council had challenged them to produce, and he did so.

Bath Preservation Trust to the Town Clerk of Bath, 21 May 1962:

As requested in your letter I am handing to you with this letter the sketch plan embodying the suggestions of my Trustees for the completion of the east side of Beaufort Square and the redevelopment of the west side of Barton Street. . . . My Trustees have approved this sketch plan in principle but in detail it is of course capable of alteration in accordance with the suggestions of the Planning Committee. The plan allows for the retention of the façade and front rooms of the present No 5 Beaufort Square and the modernisation of the back rooms. The plan is submitted in the belief that it presents an economically viable scheme for dealing with the area, and it is suggested that it should be put to open tender to be built to the specifications and under the supervision of the architect Ernest Tew, the tenders taking the form of an offer of ground rent.

Mr Herbert Fuller to the Editor of the Bath Evening Chronicle, *2 June:*
Since I saw you on the 28 May I have come across two more Bath Directories.

The Bath Directory for 1837 published by H. Silverthorne (he was librarian at the Royal Literary Institution) contains 'an alphabetical arrangement of the names and places of abode of the inhabitants'. Beaufort is used for this square . . . On page 212, under 'Supply of Water in case of Fire'— situations of the plugs connected with the various water-pipes—one of these plugs is demonstrated to be located opposite 9, Beaufort Square.

Town Clerk of Bath to Bath Preservation Trust, 27 June:
I write to say that the plans . . . were submitted to the Planning (Development) Sub-Committee . . . who decided to recommend the Planning Committee to instruct the City Planning Officer to prepare an estimate of the cost of carrying out the proposed development and that the Corporation's Valuer . . . be instructed to assess the rent income which we were likely to receive if such development were carried out by the Corporation. . . . In the meantime can you give me an indication as to what capital sum the Trust would expect to pay to the Corporation in the event of it being possible to carry out the scheme proposed by the Trust?

This letter also informed the Preservation Trust that the developer who had originally been interested in taking a lease on the site, the Bath firm of C. H. Beazer & Sons Ltd, had decided that Mr Tew's sketch plan was too expensive for them and they were no longer interested in the site.

The news that the Council itself might undertake the development, and the new challenge to name the sum that they were ready to contribute, put the Preservation

Trust on their mettle and they took some time to think the matter out.

Mr Herbert Fuller to Bath Preservation Trust, 21 August 1962:

I have been permitted to see the original lease, dated 4 March 1865, when the Trustees of St John's Hospital let to the Bath Theatre Royal Company, Limited, the Green in Beaufort Square. In this indenture all references to the name of this Square are spelt with a 't'—Bcaufort.

Bath Preservation Trust to Town Clerk of Bath, 1 October 1962:

Thank you for your letter of 27 June. . . . In reply to your question about the sum which the Trustees would expect to be able to contribute, it is assumed that the Beaufort Square façade could be restored on the same basis as the restoration work in the Circus, and the Trustees would expect to make a substantial contribution to the cost of the additional decorative work required to match the other buildings in the Square.

Town Clerk of Bath to Bath Preservation Trust, 24 October:

In submitting details to the Corporation's Valuer, the Planning (Development) Sub-Committee authorised me to inform him that the Trust's contribution to this scheme would be £10,000.

Bath Preservation Trust to Town Clerk of Bath, 5 November 1962:

Thank you for your letter of 24 October which I placed before my Trustees . . .
I was instructed to write to you pointing out that the figure of £10,000 has not been authorised by them but that their undertaking remains as stated in my letter to you of 1 October 1962 in my second paragraph, i.e. It is assumed that the Beaufort Square façade could be restored on the same basis as the restoration work in the Circus, and the

Trustees would expect to make a substantial contribution
to the cost of the additional decorative work required to
match the other buildings in the Square. The Trustees
are most anxious to see the complete restoration of Beaufort
Square and trust that problems involved in the undertaking
can be satisfactorily resolved. They are convinced that the
scheme prepared by Mr Tew is economically viable provided that the restoration of the frontage is treated as a
separate cost.

*Bath Preservation Trust to Municipal Charities, 27 Nov-
ember:*

I am being pressed by the Bath and Bristol local papers
to make a statement on the position reached in regard to
the proposed restoration of the east end of Beaufort Square.
I am enclosing a rough draft of the statement and should
be grateful if you could advise me whether the Trustees
of the Municipal Charities would object to it being published.

Draft:

. . . The restoration of the east end of the Square must go
hand in glove with the proper maintenance of the other
houses in the Square. Certain difficulties have now arisen
because of the poor state of some of these houses under the
area railings which must involve the owners of the property
in very heavy expenditure. . . . A solution of this new
problem must be sought before progress can be made in
regard of the Trustee's scheme for the east end of the
Square.

*Bath Municipal Charities to Bath Preservation Trust, 28
November:*

It was kind of you to send me a draft of the Bath Preservation Trust's proposed statement on Beaufort Square about
which I have spoken to the Chairman. While the Trustees
do not necessarily agree with the statement, they have no
objection at all to its being published as coming from the
Bath Preservation Trust.

Town Clerk of Bath to Bath Preservation Trust, 20 December 1962:

I write to inform you that the Planning Committee approved a Recommendation of their Development Sub-Committee that there should be a joint meeting between representatives of the Bath Preservation Trust. The Municipal Charities and the Planning (Development) Sub-Committee for the purpose of discussing the future of Beaufort Square.

At this meeting the City Council informed the Preservation Trust that, even with the contribution the Trust expected to be able to make, the Council did not find the prospect of doing the development itself attractive.

The Trust was thus thrown back on its own resources, if it hoped to be able to do anything.

Bath Preservation Trust to Town Clerk of Bath, 27 February 1963:

The architect responsible for the design for the rebuilding of the east end of Beaufort Square, Mr Ernest M. Tew, has consulted with a quantity surveyor about the probable cost of carrying out his design and he reports that it would be between £77,500 and £80,000: included in these figures is the extra cost of the doric treatment of Beaufort Square which he estimates at £4,000. These figures are exclusive of professional fees.

Mr Tew points out that whatever building is erected on this site, providing it is restricted to three storeys, is bound to have roughly the same cubic content as his sketch design and therefore the cost would approximate to the cost he quotes. My Trustees ask me to enquire whether the Council would be willing to let the site to another developer who would be prepared to build Mr Tew's design on the same terms which were previously offered by the Council to Messrs C. H. Beazer Ltd?

It was at this point that Mr John Cowley, principal of a local estate agent, Crisp's Estate Agency, stepped in and solved the matter to the contentment of all concerned and to his own proper advantage. He introduced

a London developer, the Bampton Property Group Ltd,
to the Bath Preservation Trust, and the Trust introduced the developer to the City Council.

*Crisp's Estate Agency to Bath Preservation Trust, 4
April 1963:*

I am very pleased to inform you that Mr Parrett, a director
of the above company, telephoned me this afternoon to
tell me that they were definitely prepared to proceed with
the redevelopment of Beaufort Square on the terms discussed. . . . You may possibly consider that you would like to
communicate to the Town Clerk at the earliest opportunity. . . .

Town Clerk of Bath to Bath Preservation Trust, 5 April:
In the circumstances I now await the receipt of the proposals anticipated by Messrs Crisp's Estate Agency.

*Bampton Property Group to Bath Preservation Trust,
April:*

We write to confirm that we would like to take a lease on
the site of Beaufort Square and Barton Street, Bath, subject
to contract. We understand that such a lease would be for
ninety-nine years at the rent of £100 per annum with a
rent review at the seventh year. We further understand that
no rent will be payable for the first year. We confirm that
we will be prepared to develop this site in the style and
manner outlined on the drawings prepared by your architect Mr Tew.

Contracts were exchanged and the detailed drawings
were drawn up, but another obstacle appeared. It is not
always greed or inertia that stands in the way of preservation: it is sometimes preservation.

*Bath Preservation Trust to the Town Clerk of Bath, 31
March 1964:*

It has been suggested that there is a hitch in the plans. . . .
I should be grateful if you could let me know the present
position. . . .

Town Clerk of Bath to Bath Preservation Trust, 3 April 1964:

The Ministry of Public Buildings and Works have indicated that the Ancient Monuments Board for England have now approved the scheduling of the monument to be known as 'The Roman Baths and Site of Roman Town'. One of the areas to be scheduled is . . . part of the site agreed to be let to the Bampton Property Group. The effect of the notice is that . . . no person shall execute . . . any work for the purpose of demolishing, removing or repairing any part of the monument . . . until the expiration of three months' notice.

The notice was given, and in due course the proposed work was approved.

Bampton Property Group to Bath Preservation Trust, 22 February 1965:

I am sure you will be pleased to hear that at long last we have been able to sign a contract for the rebuilding work on the East side of Beaufort Square.

And so the work began. The first stage was of course the clearing of the site and the digging of foundations, during which the whole of No 5 except the façade, which was virtually the only valuable part, was with general agreement demolished. In view of what is said elsewhere in this book about façades, the next episode in the history will be allowed to speak for itself from the correspondence.

Town Clerk of Bath to Bath Preservation Trust, 19 July 1965:

5 Beaufort Square

I write to inform you that the Planning Committee . . . received a report from the City Engineer indicating

(a) that he was not satisfied about the stability of the front wall of these premises, nor about the method used to tie the wall to the new floor levels;

(b) that the side wall of the premises which adjoins the

Theatre Royal is leaning outwards approximately nine inches.

The report also refers to the question of rebuilding what remains of the existing premises and thus avoid the possibility of excessive future maintenance costs or, at the worst, the collapse of the facing stonework.

'What remains of the existing premises' was the façade.

Bath Preservation Trust to Bampton Property Group, 4 August 1965:

I have had a letter from the Town Clerk of Bath which reads as follows. . . .

Bampton Property Group to Bath Preservation Trust, 5 August:

I find the contents of this extremely distressing and I have asked Mr Tew to see me. . . . I am sure you are aware that we have done our very best to comply with the wishes of the Bath Preservation Trust and local feelings by making a strong endeavour to save 'Christmas card cottage'.

I am not completely satisfied with the way this work has proceeded, and considerable extra costs have of course been incurred. It may be regrettably that the answer is to rebuild the front wall, but again this would be a very expensive solution, since we have already incurred the cost of supporting the building for a considerable length of time. I will, however, keep you fully informed of the position.

Bath Preservation Trust to Mr Tew, 14 August:

I am writing to apologise for the trouble I caused, however unintentionally, by sending the Town Clerk's letter to the Trust, about Beaufort Square, to the Bampton Property Group.

As the letter clearly should not have been sent to the Trust, who are not concerned with it, I assumed that it was merely an attempt to identify the Trust with the propping up of dangerous façades. And so, in acknowledging it, I said that I would pass it on to those concerned.

Bath Preservation Trust to E. N. Underwood, Consulting Engineer, Past President of the Institution of Structural Engineers, Bristol, 11 September 1965:

The contractors have reported that they are unable to insure the front wall, i.e. the façade in question, due to its instability. It is understood that the rubble backing of the wall is in bad condition due to

(a) crumbling mortar; and

(b) lack of bond between it and the ashlar facing.

The Trust would therefore be grateful if you would make an independent inspection and report with a view to answering the following questions:—

1 Can this wall be repaired and made safe in such a way as to satisfy the normal requirements of an insurance company and/or mortgagee for ninety-nine years?

2 If the answer to 1 is yes:—

    (a) what treatment would you recommend? and

    (b) what approximate costs would be involved?

If you are able to accept this commission for the Bath Preservation Trust, I shall be glad if you could arrange to let us have a report as soon as possible. . . .

E. N. Underwood & Partners to the Bath Preservation Trust, 17 September:

I found the original facing in excellent condition and undisturbed except for a crack over the door opening and one or two minor cracks under the windows. These cracks are of very long standing and have not been caused by the present reconstruction of the interior.

Internally, the old wall was found to be in first-class condition considering its age. I would have no doubts about its lasting qualities, especially if the property is to be occupied and kept warm and dry.

It is noticeable that considerable under-pinning of the internal piers between the windows has taken place and that this has been done skilfully and without any damage to the remaining masonry. The whole object of the reconstruction has been to relieve the outer wall of any superimposed loading, and in fact the new reinforced concrete structure within the property has been used as a frame from which the old wall is now steadied.

To put things in proper proportion, it should be emphasised that the facing which I have been asked to consider represents only a small part of the perimeter of the building and carries no responsibility for the stability of the building, so that in considering the lasting qualities of the property as a whole this facing can be discounted.

I can see no reason therefore, if normal maintenance is carried out, why the wall should not still be there at the end of another century.

Bath Preservation Trust to Bampton Property Group, 22 September:

The Trustees welcomed the report as a complete justification of their original contention that the façade should be preserved. They instructed me to send a copy to the Town Clerk of Bath and to the Minister of Housing and Local Government on whose authority the decision as to the retention of the façade rests.

The Trustees wish me again to advise you of their appreciation of the cooperation of your firm in this matter.

Bampton Property Group to Bath Preservation Trust, 21 September:

I will await hearing from you before I comment on the report although I must say at this stage that I do not clearly understand the last two paragraphs of the letter from Mr E. N. Underwood.

Mr E. N. Underwood to Bath Preservation Trust, 7 October 1965:

I refer to your telephone conversation of yesterday and to your reference to the last paragraphs in my report dated 17 September 1965. I confirm and I repeat it that there is nothing I wish to alter or add to these two paragraphs. I feel that the proper approach is to take every opportunity of tying the facings of the wall by means of nails shot into the facing stone which would secure galvanized or non-corrosive ties in exactly the manner which Mr Tew has already used to secure the cornice-stones; but my inspection of the building suggests that there is no need for this to be done for a very long time. . . . The facing, I repeat, is undisturbed by the present operation, has only suffered one or two minor settlement cracks in the distant past and is stable. I fear that any interference in the facing with the object of making it more secure may well have the opposite effect.

Councillor John McCloskey reported in the 'Bath and Wilts Chronicle', *6 October:*

If the Bath Preservation Trust have any sites they want preserved in future they should be told to 'do it themselves'. . . . Accidents have happened in a number of cases.

Messrs E. N. Underwood & Partners to Bath Preservation Trust, 14 October:

As you will know, I met Mr Tew on the site of Beaufort Square yesterday afternoon so that we could jointly discuss with the City Engineer and his chief Building Inspector the problems which they felt might arise in preserving the façade of the above. A most friendly discussion ensued and all realised that, if more ties between the façade and back wall could be obtained, then the likelihood of any future damage or deterioration of the façade would be very remote indeed. It transpired that Mr Tew was in fact removing all the existing timber window frames completely and this afforded a wonderful opportunity to insert additional metal ties rag-bolted into the masonry on the inside and to the façade on the outside, so that the entire tie arrangement would be buried behind the window frame and internal plaster. . . . Mr Tew willingly undertook to include these ties and with this promise the City Engineer was much reassured about the lasting qualities of the building and now has no anxieties that the façade needs to be removed.

Bath Preservation Trust to E. N. Underwood & Partners, 18 October:

I am very grateful indeed for your letter . . . and for all the trouble you have taken over investigating this case on behalf of the Bath Preservation Trust. These sentiments will be warmly echoed by all the Trustees.

The solution that you have agreed with the City Engineer and Building Inspector seems an admirable one from every point of view, and I am now hopeful that the Trust's objective of preserving the façade of this house will be accomplished without encountering further difficulties.

Bampton Property Group to Mr Tew, 18 November 1965:

I note that you will be letting me have the designs for shop fronts [in Barton Street] in the near future and it occurs to me that the Bath Preservation Trust has collected a certain amount of money for 5 Beaufort Square and they have always been willing to assist us to some extent. Whilst it would not be possible to accept a lump sum from them, I have always been agreeable to their undertaking a particular item within the development. I know that shop fronts are one of the things which they feel fairly strongly about and in view of the considerable additional cost which we have incurred on the whole development, I wondered if you would like to let me have your view of asking them to pay for the proposed shop fronts.

Bath Preservation Trust to Mr Tew, 20 December 1965:

I brought this matter before the Trustees at their December meeting. They are keenly aware of the importance of the shop fronts in this building . . . but they regret that such a grant for commercial purposes is outside the scope of the Articles of Association governing the Trust. The Trustees recalled their original offer to contribute to the cost of the decorative features necessary to link the new building with the existing houses of the Square, and to say that they are still prepared to consider a grant for such a specific purpose.

Bath Preservation Trust to Bampton Property Group, 7 October 1966:

The Beaufort Square building appears to be reaching completion and it is winning favourable comment on all sides, even from those who initially derided the plan.

We would like to give, with your kind permission and co-operation, a small house-warming party to celebrate its opening and will be grateful to be allowed the use of one of the shops for the purpose.

The party was held and the shops and flats in due course let. Altogether the capital cost of the development was £90,000, and in the end the Bath Preservation Trust did not have to contribute anything at all, thus achieving a first rate Stukeley. The Bampton Property Group holds the land on a ninty-nine year lease with a ground rent of £100 a year, renewable after seven years.

The final result of the exercise is extremely pleasing when seen from Beaufort Square and there is no doubt that the employment of an adaptable architect, able to build a correct Georgian copy for the Preservation Trust (Plate 2) and to build commercial for the developer (Plate 3) has led to a result satisfactory to all those whose satisfaction was necessary to its achievement. The early eighteenth century façades, one genuine, one replica, are in fact simply the backs of shops and a *pizzeria;* if you look into what should be living-room windows, you see egg boxes and saucepans stacked. Some may worry about the aesthetic morality or moral aesthetics of this sort of preservation: but others will enjoy the scene and say, why not? In any case, by securing the plugging of this one key gap, the Bath Preservation Trust have also secured the survival of a complete and pleasant early Georgian environment which would otherwise certainly have been lost.

THE HALL, GOSPORT

Not every preservation battle ends in success, and not every one is fought by a well-founded and well-organised society. The story that follows is one of failure, but is noteworthy because of the courage and ingenuity of the young and solitary protagonist.

From the monthly leaflet of Holy Trinity Church, Gosport, January 1965:

The Hall

The departments of the Borough Council which have been occupying The Hall have moved out to new quarters and the house is now empty. The latest information is that it is to be demolished within a matter of weeks, so another landmark of the old town will disappear. It has stood for just over a hundred and fifty years and has had a chequered existence. It was the first vicarage; it has housed more than one Gosport family; Mrs Briggs—whom many of us remember—lived there for many years; Miss Briggs converted it into a guest house; Ultra Ltd, occupied it as their first factory in Gosport; and finally the Borough Engineer and the Parks Department have been using it.

A part of the land upon which it stands has been assigned by the Town Planning Authority for the new vicarage as soon as the site has been cleared, so the development in this direction will ensue. How long it will be before this new vicarage is built I would not care to prophesy.

The building in question was a sober three-storeyed house of the early nineteenth century which had contained a fine spiral staircase and some good panelling and fireplaces, but had fallen into disrepair. It was already partly surrounded by very tall modern blocks: see the photograph in plate 4. A further notion of the prevailing standards in Gosport at the time can be obtained from plates 5 and 6.

Portsmouth Evening News, 5 January 1965:

Gosport demolition halted by Ministry men. Call wreckers off. A few hours after demolition contractors had started stripping slates from the roof of the deserted Hall Guest House, Gosport, they were called off the job. It was discovered that the building was listed as being of historic and architectural interest and could not be pulled down without ministerial permission. . . . For more than ten years Gosport Borough Council had been under the impression that it had authority to demolish it so the Parish of Holy Trinity could built a new vicarage there.

Portsmouth Evening News, 6 January:

Historic building saved by sixth-former. Demolition halted at Gosport. Responsible for halting the demolition of The Hall Guest House, listed for preservation as a building of historic interest, at Gosport was sixteen-year-old Stephen Weeks . . . a sixth-form student at Portsmouth Grammar School. He is studying modern languages as a prelude to becoming an architect and is highly critical of the Gosport Borough Council's policy on old buildings.

The Times, 7 January:

Youth blocks demolition by Council. Portsmouth, January 6. A Gosport schoolboy aged sixteen has stopped Gosport Borough Council from demolishing The Hall Guest House overlooking Portsmouth Harbour by personally going to the Ministry of Housing and Local Government. He is Stephen Weeks. . . . He discovered on Monday that the Council had not received permission to demolish the building, which is over 150 years old and is scheduled[1] as of historic and architectural interest. 'I went to the London offices of the Ministry on Monday to tell them of the position. At once they contacted the Borough Engineer and ordered demolition to cease', he said today. 'On Monday I am meeting the Ministry's Chief Investigator for Ancient Monuments[1] on the site and I shall also be showing him a number of other historic features in the town which are worth preserving. I feel this is necessary as the local council do not seem to have much regard for preserving buildings and sites which are part of their heritage. Since 1948 no fewer than fifty-six old buildings have been demolished and I feel this must stop'.

[1] i.e. listed.
[1] i.e. of historic buildings.

Support in Town

He added 'I am not alone in this fight—I have had support from other people in the town as well as from Councillor Wallis of the Portsmouth Museum Society'. The Borough Engineer . . . said the Council had been under the impression that it had permission to demolish the building. Slates were being taken off the roof when work was halted by the Ministry'.

The *New Daily*, 8 January:

'Man versus the Machine. How helpless the individual so often feels in the face of the all powerful state machine! A thinking adult is but one fifty-six millionth part of the government of the nation and an insignificant percentage of even his local government. So overwhelmed are many faint hearts by the bureaucracy that few bother to kick against the pricks. It is therefore heartening—indeed inspiring— to read of the case where a sixteen-year-old schoolboy of Gosport stopped the Borough Council from pulling down The Hall Guest House which is 150 years old and has been scheduled as an historic monument . . . While the lone protester may deplore the apathy of those around him he can take some comfort from the fact that throughout history the protest movements for greater social progress have always been started by one or a few stalwart and determined individuals. Once they have accepted the responsibility, others will jump on the band-wagon.

Daily Telegraph, 9 January:

Stephen Weeks, the Gosport schoolboy who has stopped the local council from demolishing an old building, yesterday spent an hour showing an Investigator from the Ministry of Housing and Local Government around the town. On Monday the boy went to the Ministry after learning that Gosport Council did not have permission to pull down The Hall overlooking Portsmouth Harbour. The Ministry telephoned instructions to stop demolition work. Yesterday the boy met Mr Antony Dale, Chief Investigator Ancient Monuments. Together they crouched over broken tiles and plaster,

[1] i.e. listed as a building of historic or architectural interest.

and had a look over the 130-year-old three-storey house which was until recently Corporation offices.

Beautiful staircase, balustrade missing

They went up the beautifully curved staircase now sadly lacking a balustrade and looked over many of the rooms. Then the boy took Mr Dale for a brisk tramp through the centre of the town to see other historic features which he thinks worth preserving. . . . Mr Dale, who later met Gosport Council officials, said: 'I can make no comment. I can only report to the Minister. I have never known a young lad to have such a detailed knowledge of this kind. . .' The boy said: 'I have already had many letters from local people pledging their support to this campaign, but nothing from the Council. I am writing to the Town Clerk offering to address the Council: perhaps some kind of policy can be adopted to prevent further historic buildings disappearing'.

Portsmouth News, 9 January:

Top Level Talks on Fate of THAT House at Gosport

A conference was held at Gosport today at which the future of The Hall Guest House was debated. The Borough Council's Finance Committee has been considering the financial implications of halting the demolition and the cost to the rate-payers should the Minister order the reparation of the building.

Letters to the Editor

'In the late extra edition of the "Evening News" of January 5 were two photographs, one of Fareham's gas works and the other of a roofless old ruin. It was difficult to decide which of the two was more ugly and yet to my horror I learn that one of them is supposed to be an object of historic interest and, wait for it . . . architectural beauty. In the "News" of January 6, I read that Master Stephen Weeks' efforts have held up the demolition of this old ruin known as The Hall, because of some trifling permisison which has to be received from the Ministry or Hampshire County Council. . . . Master Weeks is entitled to his opinion as to what constitutes Gosport's heritage, but of the fifty-six buildings demolished in this area since 1948, I understand that they were composed of slum tenement houses and rotting cottages, derelict warehouses and a mid-nineteenth-century steam laundry. Their demolition has transformed this area and made way for modern old people's homes and much needed residential accommodation which have blended in with Holy Trinity Church to make this part of the town one of the most pleasant areas in Gosport, far from the slum that it was. Instead of Gosport Borough Council being criticised for its action in clearing up the mess which formed Gosport's waterfront, I feel it should be praised for its realistic and progressive policy towards these areas which are eye-sores. I would be the first to fight against the demolition of buildings of true historic or architectural interest, but the saving of any of the buildings quoted by Master Weeks would be preserving rotten and inferior examples of architecture of an age best forgotten as far as Gosport is concerned. Graham J. Hewitt, Councillor.'

With reference to your papers of January 5 and 6 concerning The Hall Guest House, it would be enlightening to know what is "historic" about this place, which should have been pulled down years ago. It is nothing but a dump of brickwork in a very bad state of repair and is an eye-sore to the growing and enterprising town of Gosport.

Leader: Gosport's blushes in a good cause
Few tears are likely to be shed at Gosport or elsewhere should the partial demolition of the 150-year-old Hall Guest House be eventually completed. But the incident will have been worth every blush of embarrassment if a somewhat apathetic public is jerked into a realisation of what can happen. All about us fine trees are being swathed, nature reserves eroded, familiar paths built over and every spark of interest or individuality threatened with extinction by the advancing tide of bricks and cement. . . . In Gosport nothing priceless has been lost. The anxiety is that through a misunderstanding a Ministry Preservation Order had not been observed. The Borough has much reason for pride in its redevelopment achievements, but the new toothy skyline of tall buildings has as much individuality as a leg of a centipede. . . Having to be put right by a boy of sixteen was a discomfiture which Gosport must show to be undeserved.

Sunday Telegraph, 10 January:

The boy who challenged his elders
Stephen reasons his case firmly and strongly: 'I always had an interest in the preservation of ancient things. At first I was keen on Roman antiquities. But then I realised I had a duty to do. Saving Roman stuff is all very fine but there's a crisis in eighteenth and nineteenth century buildings—they are being knocked down all the time.' So he buckled down to work and formed the South Hampshire Trust. . . . Both adults and young people showed interest and though their first effort ended in failure, it proved an invaluable practice round for the current battle. They had tried to save the King's Store House in Portsmouth which was being demolished so that the power station could be erected. The Trust had managed to postpone demolition for six weeks before it was decided that the building did not have enough architectural merit to remain standing at the cost of finding a new site for the power station. All this time Stephen's classmates looked on with amused interest: 'They used to think I was a bit of a nut', he remembers: but gradually their curiosity brought them round and now many of them are as dedicated as I am.' It is not just his classmates at Portsmouth Grammar School who have been fired by his obvious enthusiasm. Last summer he and his Trust started excavations at the ancient Fontley Iron Mills. . . . At first the excavators had an audience of young toughs who jeered and sneered. 'We just ignored them', said Stephen, 'and after a couple of hours leaning on walls they started to help us. By the end of the summer we had thirty people helping at Fontley after starting from scratch'.

Guardian, 11 January:

Schoolboy's initiative, by John Grigg
Stephen Weeks, a sixteen-year-old schoolboy in Gosport, has set an example which should be followed throughout the country. . . . Unfortunately in appealing to the Ministry of Housing he is taking his case to a body whose credentials are deeply suspect. Under the Ministry's aegis, the wholesale destruction of beautiful or interesting buildings is going on all the time. Aesthetic and historic considerations are being

recklessly sacrificed to short term economic requirements.
Brick by brick, stone by stone, the distinctive charm and
character of our country are being thrown away. Instead, an
inferior version of America is being created.

Portsmouth Evening News, 11 January:

Members of the South East Hampshire Area Planning Committee today decided to urge the County Planning Committee to support the demolition of The Hall Guest House,
Gosport. . . . The Chairman said: 'The Borough Council
did not intend to violate the preservation order. The work
was begun under the mistaken impression that the building
was included in another permit from the Minister.' Councillor R. A. Kirkin, a Gosport representative, said: 'It has
always been the intention of the Borough Council to develop
the whole of this area, which has been going on for a
considerable number of years. The Hall itself has fallen
into a very bad state of disrepair because there seemed little
object in pouring a lot of money into a building that was
going to be demolished.'

Portsmouth Evening News, 12 January:

**Ministry blamed for Hall mix-up. Gosport 'held up to
ridicule.'** The Ministry of Housing and Local Government
was blamed last night for the misunderstanding which led
to the start on demolishing The Hall Guest House, Gosport. The Borough Council was told that a decision had
been made and noted at the Ministry, but it had never
been passed on to the Council. Not one Councillor spoke in
favour of retaining the 150-year-old building, the demolition of which was stopped on order from the Ministry after
sixteen-year-old Portsmouth Grammar School student
Stephen Weeks had called attention to it being a building
scheduled for preservation. Councillor H. Pattison com-
mented: 'I think we ought to send young Stephen Weeks
a letter congratulating him. He stopped something that was
not absolutely legal'. 'The fellow from the Ministry said
they did have a note in the Ministry that The Hall might
be preserved, but the correspondence stating this view was
never passed to Gosport', said Alderman Rogers. 'It was
the view of the Finance Committee that it was in the public

9 The Barbican, Plymouth. The modern building is old people's flats, built by a housing association.
See page 199.

10 The Motcomb Street Pantechnicon.
See page 184.

11 and 12
Magdalene
College,
Cambridge,
before.
See page 202.

interest to pull this building down. Councillor Harvey Pink: 'Who decided this place was of architectural interest in the first place? I cannot understand it'. Councillor E. T. W. Lander declared: 'This Borough has been held up to ridicule in the national press and we have been made monkeys of by a boy of sixteen'. Councillor G. J. Hewitt refuted the suggestion that the Council had been held up to ridicule: 'I think the people have enough common sense to decide the matter themselves', he remarked.

'Awful'

Alderman C. P. Osborn said: 'The Ministry should be held up to ridicule because of this awful business'. Alderman Rogers summed up: 'This Council has nothing to be ashamed of. One has only to look at where we have fallen over backwards to preserve buildings where there has been architectural merit. One has only to look at The Crescent for that. I was born in Gosport, right in the centre of this area—my family probably goes back farther in this area than of any other member of this Council. To be quite frank it was a dump, and the sooner it was pulled down the better.'

Letters to the Editor:

I was delighted to read that Gosport Council has been halted by a schoolboy . . . Old Gosportian.
Whatever the merits of the old Hall as a specimen of architecture worthy of preservation, it is unfair of Councillor Hewitt to try to make fun of it as a 'roofless old ruin' when the very body which has reduced it to this state is Gosport Council.

Daily Mirror, 12 January:

Stephen, 16, wins TV job

Schoolboy Stephen Weeks, whose fight to stop a Council demolishing an old building was supported by the Ministry of Housing, has won a TV job. Stephen, 16, will report on historical buildings for the Southern Television magazine programme "Day by Day". Stephen, of Gosport, Hants., conducted his original campaign against Gosport Council.

Portsmouth Evening News, Letters to the Editor, 15 January:

I first paid a visit to The Hall nearly forty years ago in order to give a message to my girl guide mistress, Miss Briggs . . . 'L. Freebody'

Why can't this town, unlike neighbouring old Portsmouth, see that to give future generations a clear and accurate picture of the exciting, confusing drunken place that gave shelter to our Jack Tars means preserving not only a few hand-picked 'period houses' and other choice relics, but also some of the muddled, rambling old properties around which the town grew up. It is high time that someone with a little more imagination and real understanding of Gosport's 'bad old days' took a hand in its planning, and S. Weeks has certainly tried. Signed: Young Preservationist.

Portsmouth Evening News, 20 January:

Recording a Christmas visit to Stanley House[1] about sixty years ago, Mrs Childs writes: 'My chief recollections are of the magnificent circular staircase and the glasshouse on the roof where many ships in Spithead and the harbour were pointed out to us.' She still has an Evening News cutting of 1888 giving an account of her parents' marriage from Stanley House. 'It is quite long since it was something of an event in Gosport at that time", she writes. "This was because twin Lapthorn brothers married two Nicholson sisters—in other words the yachts married the sails".'[2]

The Hall was in due course completely demolished, and its site remains vacant. The fuss did, in Mr Weeks's opinion, contribute to preventing the demolition of the Vicarage, a companion house built about forty years before the Hall, but not to any general improvement in local standards.

[1] As The Hall was then known.

[2] Ratsey & Lapthorn were the leading sailmakers and Camper & Nicholson were the leading yachtbuilders of England from the late nineteenth century to the Second World War.

THE ENFIELD ROAD

The North London suburb of Enfield is one of those villages which got encapsulated as London spread. The main shopping street runs north towards a fine old church; north of the church again there is an area of graveyard, of shady walks under immense trees, of cottages, a school, private gardens, public gardens, low walls; in a word, just that sort of accretion of the ages which makes a village a village and a town a town. Photographs at plates 7 and 8. The story that follows is a village story; it could as well have happened in a rural village as in a suburban one, and stories like it do happen in rural villages all the time.

In the late 1950s the Enfield Borough Council conceived the notion of pedestrianising the shopping street. This would have been an admirable notion, but for the fact that it could only be done by building a ring road from the south of it right round the outside and cutting across this pleasant and peaceful area north of the church. The lie of the land can be seen from the map on p. 164.

From the minutes of the Town Planning Committee of Enfield Borough Council, 14 December 1960:

The Borough Engineer reported on the traffic problems obtaining in the town centre. . . . In view of the pressure being exerted by prospective developers and the likelihood of further planning applications resulting in appeals which might in the absence of a 'master plan' prejudice the future of the town centre, it was essential that an early decision should be made. The Committee recommended . . . that the Borough Engineer be authorised to negotiate with prospective developers with a view to any redevelopment of the town centre being carried out in a manner to conform with the proposals now approved in principle.'

i.e. the ring road cutting right through the mini-Arcadia by the church.

On 1 June 1961 a conference was held at the Gas Offices Lecture Hall in Enfield of organisations and

THE ENFIELD ROAD PROJECT

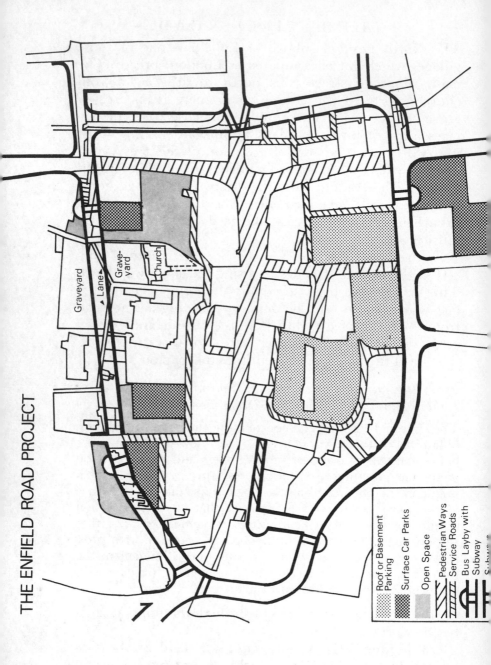

Graveyard

Lane

Grave-
yard

Church

Roof or Basement
Parking

Surface Car Parks

Open Space

Pedestrian Ways

Service Roads

Bus Layby with
Subway

Subway

individuals interested in the Enfield town plan at which a campaign committee known at first as the 'Town Plan Working Party' was elected. On 14 March 1963 the Town Plan Working Party met the Area Planning Officer of the Borough Council, and the County Engineer. The Working Party expressed the alarm with which the town plan was viewed by a large cross-section of Enfield opinion. The Area Planning Officer replied that he had been fully aware of the problem for many years, and of the local residents' objections which had been sent to County level by the Borough. He told the Working Party that an enquiry would be held without fail by the Minister.

Minutes of the Town Plan Working Party, 11 May 1963:
It was thought 'the Opposition' should have an official and inspiriting title . . . e.g. 'The Campaign Committee for Revision of Enfield's Town Plan'. Headed writing paper should be printed when the title had been decided upon.

Another conference, by now of twenty-six Enfield Societies, was held on 29 April 1963, at which it was urged that 'the Town Plan should be attacked at the weakest point, which is the northern part of the plan.' This conference also decided 'that it is absolutely essential to have professional counsel at the public enquiry. The Chairman gave the figure of £500 for council's fees, and the conference passed a resolution . . . that the fighting fund be instituted.'

At another conference, the fourth, on 11 June 1963, Mr C, the Branch Manager of — Bank, was adopted as Treasurer and the title 'Save Enfield Campaign' was decided upon. The Working Party was renamed the 'Action Committee'.

Minutes of a meeting of the Action Committee, 2 August 1963:

The proposed exhibit for the town show. A letter from the Town Clerk was read suggesting the Action Committee should arrange an exhibit at the town show in September to show alternate schemes to the town plan as produced and approved by the Borough Council. . . . This was agreed unanimously. . . . The Chairman suggested the sum of £50 should be spent on the exhibition; this was agreed. Volunteers to man the stand. . . . The twelve ladies who have offered to sell produce in the market for the fighting fund might help.

Minutes of a meeting of the Action Committee, 12 September 1963:

The Treasurer reported £279 in the Fighting Fund. . . . The Chairman moved a warm vote of thanks to Mr — for all his work in getting the stand ready at such short notice. It was decided to authorise at the next meeting the sum of two guineas to be spent on a gift token for the helpers.

Minutes of a meeting of the Action Committee, 31 January 1964:

The Treasurer reported that the Fighting Fund stood at £298. . . . It was emphasised that the campaign's plan for the enquiry must be absolutely ready. After considerable discussion it was agreed to find a solicitor living outside the Borough but possessing certain knowledge of local matters. . . . The Chairman warned the members of the danger of too many groups voicing the same opposition at the enquiry. . . . Petition: all roads are being canvassed in the Borough . . . and nearly all roads have been covered.

Minutes of Action Committee, 9 March 1964:

Mr —'s reported estimates for our opposition at the public enquiry were considered but the figure of £600 was thought quite out of the Committee's range. His offer of help was declined with thanks. . . . The Hon Treasurer gave a considered opinion that the Campaign cannot possibly expect £1,000 for its opposition. . . . Balance in hand: £302.

Action Committee Minutes, 7 April 1964:

It was felt strongly that Mr —, our solicitor, should meet the Committee as soon as possible to learn all the many points of opposition . . . The Secretary promised to find details of a Counsel, who it is said is a fighter and has won many a case for bodies such as the Save Enfield campaign.

Action Committee Minutes, 11 May 1964:

Mr — explained the organisation of the petition and his method of checking the possible duplication of signatures. He reported that 9,752 unduplicated signatures were registered to date. Also that 624 signatures were collected in the market on May 2. . . . Mr — agreed to mark out with posts the position of the ring road through the churchyard. . . . The Hon Treasurer reported that the Fighting Fund stood at £421 with an anonymous gift of £100 and about £10 collected in the market place on May 2. The display on that occasion cost £6 8s. 6d. The bill for the three banners had not yet been received.

Action Committee, 19 June 1964:

The Chairman reported on the first meeting with the new solicitor for the Campaign, Mr David Napley. He stressed the fact that success at the public enquiry depended simply on money . . . at least £1,000 to £1,500 was needed to put our case to the Inspector. Discussion followed on ways and means to obtain more donations to the Fighting Fund. . . . It was decided to write to Mr Napley asking him to act for the Campaign, explain the present shortage of funds, but ask him to study the documents he asked for and to let us know the cost of expert witnesses. . . . The Chairman emphasised the importance of the Campaign remaining strictly non-political. But we can be grateful, he said, for any help any party can give privately. Mr — said he has had no help from local political parties at all. The Honorary Treasurer reported that the fund stood at £468. The Chairman told the conference that success at the enquiry will depend on a well-planned showing by the Campaign. We must be legally represented and be represented also by expert witnesses to achieve success and all this must cost a great deal of money. . . . The Committee are advised that at least £1,500 will be needed'.

Action Committee, 17 July 1964:

More appeal letters. . . . Ask the Treasurer for petty cash.

. . . After dismissing the idea of a raffle . . . it was decided to find out details of the cost of two gross of ballpoint pens with 'Save Enfield Campaign' printed on them to sell at one shilling. . . . Ask for the Local Manufacturers Association list. . . . Appeal to the free churches by special letter. . . . A bazaar was ruled out. . . . A grand jumble sale . . . was decided upon.

Action Committee, 21 August 1964:

Treasurer's Report £774. . . . Mr — produced a ballpoint pen inscribed with 'Save Enfield Campaign' as planned. These were voted most successful. The Treasurer was authorised to pay the bill. Mr — reported that there seemed little success from his talks with the free churches and it was decided to go no further with this scheme.

Action Committee, 25 September 1964:

Has the cost of Campaign's ballpoint pens been covered? . . . Treasurer's Report: £837. . . . Messrs — and — reported on their visit to Mr Napley. He has not decided yet the best way to fight the plan. He felt it absolutely necessary to consult a traffic expert. There are two separate issues: car parking and the traffic in the town centre. He intends to visit the town later. . . . He emphasised that only one (alternative) plan should be put up at the enquiry. The original Borough Council minutes to produce the plan are needed by him and also the voting figures in the Town Ward and adjacent wards in the local elections. . . . He requires a potted history of Enfield . . . about a thousand words (it was decided to ask Mrs — to do this . . . Finally he wanted to meet all the Committee in January with representatives from some of the societies forming the Campaign.

Action Committee, 4 January 1965:

Treasurer's Report: £954. . . . The question of sending the objections of the Campaign to 'the Town Plan was discussed. Should the Action Committee send them to the Ministry or should this be done by Mr Napley? The Secretary promised to ask Mr Napley's advice on this. . . . Report on Mr Napley's visit to Enfield on December 12. He explored the area of the Town Plan very thoroughly and took photographs accompanied by members of the Action Committee.

Notes on meeting with Mr Napley, 6 January:

Money. Mr —, the traffic expert, would cost £100 to £200. Planning expert would cost £300.

Sixth conference of the Save Enfield Campaign in the Gas Board's Demonstration Theatre, 24 February 1965. Resolution:

The Action Committee understands from its Legal Adviser that the best way to fight the Borough Council's Town Plan is by tabling a constructive alternative plan. We ask the conference to accept this view and to authorise the Action Committee to proceed with a technical study to determine the most generally acceptable plan in order to preserve the historic part of the town centre, unless we are advised no traffic problem exists in the town centre.

Honorary Secretary of the Save Enfield Campaign to the Showroom Manager, Eastern Gas Board, Enfield, 26 February:

I feel I must write to you and apologise most sincerely for the state of the Gas Board's Demonstration Theatre after the conference on Wednesday last. The litter left on the floor was inexcusable and I shall make it my business to report this at the next committee meeting. Please convey to the caretaker my regrets that we kept him late.

Action Committee, 9 April 1965:

Treasurer's Report: £1,008. . . . The Chairman said that Mr B (a planning consultant) would be the key man at the enquiry. He would be the big technical stick and Napley would lean heavily on him. . . . It was reported that Iain Macleod, MP, was uninformed about the Campaign and the Secretary reported that this was definitely not the case. He had been kept informed from the first.

Action Committee, 14 May 1965:

Mr Napley seems to be apprehensive about the Campaign's

finances, but the money will be found to pay for the experts. He must understand this and produce an expert himself.

Action Committee, 10 June 1965:

It was decided to send Mr B's bill for his expenses to the Hon Treasurer. . . . The Chairman reported on Mr Napley's attitude to the alternative plan. He has assured Mr Napley that extra money will be raised somehow. He said the Committee must pay the expert witness at a fixed sum for the enquiry and any preliminary work. He thought about £1,000 might be the figure (last time the sum of £500 was mentioned). . . . It was essential to have an expert witness who would work well throughout the enquiry with Mr Napley. . . . The Chairman said that we are bound to act under Mr Napley's instructions. . . . Mr Napley's costs were discussed in some detail and it was thought that they may be £500 and more.

From Messrs —, — and Partners, Consulting Engineers to the Chairman of the Save Enfield Campaign, 10 July 1965:

We refer to the recent conversations between us and confirm that we would be pleased to advise the Save Enfield Campaign on the traffic aspects of their opposition to the proposed comprehensive redevelopment of Enfield town centre and if necessary to attend the public enquiry of the proposals. . . . For a report based on the detailed traffic analysis . . . which we would consider the best approach to your problem, we could not guarantee that the cost would not exceed your present budget of £500, including the preparation of our proof of evidence and attending the enquiry. We anticipate that the total cost would be in the range of £500 to £1,000, although £500 should be sufficient to cover the work of analysis and preparation of the report. At any rate, we would keep you informed of the cost as it was incurred and would give you earliest advice of the anticipated total cost as soon as the full content of the work is known. We trust that the above meets with your approval and that we may hear favourably from you'.

Action Committee, 9 July:

Bill for the market stall used by the Committee in 1964 was discussed, ten guineas. Treasurer's Report: £1,027. . . . The Secretary promised to find out details of a Comic Auction in St Albans which had produced a large sum for a charity. . . . .The model being made by Mr S would need to have an organised function to display it at its best, with much publicity at the same time.

Treasurer of the Save Enfield Campaign to Chairman, 16 July:

I have been seriously perturbed by the lack of response to our last letter to the various organisations which make up the Save Enfield Campaign. . . . Secondly, there was some very disturbing information that the solicitor's fees might increase from 500 guineas to an indefinite amount up to £1,000. Equally there is the estimate of the technical firm who might be able to act for us in a very satisfactory manner for approximately £500, but that this figure might of necessity have to be increased to up to £1,000. Thus there is an indefinite short-fall over our present financial resources of up to £1,000. Originally I was asked to act as Honorary Treasurer of the Campaign and the position then envisaged did not enter into the realm of the Committee being asked to undertake a joint and several liability in the respect of fees incurred through the enquiry. Since the members of the Committee are nominees of the various organisations of the Campaign I think they should not be called upon to undertake such a liability. . . . As I am a member of the Action Committee in a personal capacity I must inform you that I am not prepared to have my name included in any form of undertaking which makes me in any way jointly or separately liable for the fees etc. . . .

Secretary of Save Enfield Campaign to Chairman, 19 July:

A copy of [the Treasurer's] letter to you arrived today and we felt we must write and tell you that we both understand his attitude on this difficult question of guarantee liability. As a matter of fact we ourselves are in no position to stand guarantor for what may be a large sum.

Chairman of Save Enfield Campaign to Messrs —, — and Partners, Consulting Engineers:

An appraisal of our liabilities shows that our Legal Adviser, including attendance at the hearing, would cost something over £1,000 and there are of course other incidental expenses. The Appeal Sub-Committee report that they have to date collected £1,000 by public subscription but are not very hopeful of more than a further £500, making £1,500 in all. Although I am personally prepared to contribute a proportion of any balance that may have to be found, the other members of my Committee are not so well placed financially and are understandably not in a position to meet a substantial contribution.

In the circumstances therefore I am afraid we cannot avail ourselves of your services. . . . We are very grateful for the time you have given to this matter and are of course prepared to meet any fees we may have incurred thus far.

Messrs —, — and Partners, Consulting Engineers, to Chairman of the Save Enfield Campaign, 30 July:

If I may say so I think your Commitee has reached the right decision. . . . I appreciate the difficulties in finance and under the circumstances, much as we would like to help, regret that we cannot be of service. We shall not be making any charge for our time to date and we wish you all success in your appeal.

Town Clerk of Enfield to Chairman of Save Enfield Campaign, 30 July:

'It was noticed from the local press recently that the Save Enfield Campaign which had been organised to oppose the Council's proposals for the redevelopment of Enfield town centre had prepared an alternative scheme.

The Chairman of the Redevelopment and Town Planning Committee is anxious that members should have every opportunity of considering all possible schemes for dealing with problems in the town, and he has asked me to enquire if your organisation will be willing to disclose their suggested scheme at this stage. As you know, the Minister of Housing and Local Government is likely to hold a local enquiry into the proposals in the near future and he will no doubt wish to know the Council's views on any alternative scheme. The Chairman therefore feels that it would save considerable expense to those concerned if all relevant information were made available both to the Council and to the Inspectors now so as to avoid the necessity of asking for an adjournment of the enquiry.

Action Committee, 13 August 1965:

The Town Clerk's letter was read. . . . On the advice of Mr Napley it was decided that this meeting was most desirable providing that Mr Napley was present. . . . Important to publish the final alternative plan with the biggest bang possible and so attract more money and support.

Action Committee, 8 October 1965:

Mr S has insured the model against fire, malicious damage, etc. for £3 15s. a year; the value of the model being considered £1,000.

Action Committee, 19 November 1965:

It was decided to send 100 guineas to Mr Pullen[1] on account. . . . Final arrangements for the meeting with the Council Planning Committee had been made and Mr Napley and Mr P have agreed to be there. . . . Arrangements were then made to take the model to Mr Napley's house on Sunday afternoon on November 21. The question of presenting the model at the meeting on the 26th was discussed. Mr Napley would not commit himself until he had actually seen it on the 21st. . . . The Committee was to put on record their appreciation and sincere thanks to Mr S for his wonderful work on the model. . . .

A sketch map in the rough was passed round the Committee at this point. It was handed to the Secretary from

[1]The Campaign had by now retained Mr Granville Pullen as their planning consultant.

a Mr B (a well-wisher) who thought it might prove the solution to the town plan. Dr R (a committee member) promised to call on him and explain the latest developments and possibly ask him for a contribution to the Fighting Fund as a proof of his concern with our problems.

Agreed Press statement:

At the Civic Centre on Friday, 26 November 1965 members of the Action Committee of the Save Enfield Campaign met members of the Council's Redevelopment and Town Planning Committee in order to present their alternative proposals for the Enfield Town Centre Redevelopment Scheme.

. . . The meeting took place in a spirit of co-operation with a full and frank exchange of views and will be followed by other meetings of a similar nature so that the advantages and disadvantages of both the Council scheme and the alternative may be examined in detail. . . . At a future meeting the Council is to afford an opportunity to the Save Enfield Campaign to hear the arguments in favour of the Council scheme and to make their criticisms of it. Both sides hope that if there is any possibility of resolving their differences, this can be done before the Minister holds a public enquiry. Members of the Council expressed their appreciation to the Action Committee for the explanations of their scheme and congratulated them on the manner in which they had presented it and on the model which had been prepared by the Enfield Preservation Society.

From a Joint Report of the Borough Architect Planner and the Borough Engineer and Surveyor to the Chairman and Members of the Redevelopment and Town Planning Committee of the Enfield Borough Council, 14 June 1966:

In December 1965 the Enfield Preservation Society presented an alternative scheme for the town centre. . . . No road was provided round the north side of the town centre, thus preserving intact the open areas around the church. . . . The Committee considered that the proposals were incapable of dealing with the traffic flows involved. The service road system was inadequate and the main east-west road would have an extremely damaging effect on the aesthetics and environment of the town centre due to its large widths, function and partial elevation, and would mean accepting a major through route in the town centre for all time.

The need to minimise the visual and aural impact of the northern ring road in the central development area in the proposals was accepted by your Committee. . . . It was considered that if a visual and pedestrian link . . . could be provided it might go some way towards meeting the objections of the Enfield Preservation Society.

Consideration was therefore given to the possibility of sinking the northern ring road below ground level in the region of the church and Holly Walk. Preliminary investigation showed that it was possible to sink the road . . . to a maximum of nine feet into the ground, the additional cost being in the order of £150,000. Sinking the road by this much might not produce the desired results as the steep gradients and retaining walls involved might lead to increased traffic noise. A depression of about five feet in the road level with the land re-graded on each side to form an embankment was considered to be a more satisfactory form of treatment, since all but the tallest vehicles would be obscured and the level of traffic noise would be substantially reduced. The observations of the Enfield Preservation Society to these proposals for sinking the northern ring road. . . . were sought, but they did not consider that the proposals overcame their objection to the CDA scheme. . . . It is a matter for the Committee to decide whether they wish to proceed with the CDA proposal as now submitted to the Minister, bearing in mind that it is anticipated that modifications in land uses can be made at the time of the public enquiry and the fact that the Greater London Council officers now support the scheme and would be reluctant to see a withdrawal. Should the Council desire to proceed, decisions are required on the following matters . . . decide to ask the Minister to fix a date for the public enquiry into the CDA proposal.

Enfield Campaign, 21 December 1965:

I am writing to thank you very much indeed for the opportunity you have given us to see the excellent model which illustrates the suggestions put forward . . . for the central area of Enfield. . . . The model is being sent back to your address tomorrow.

Action Committee meeting minutes, 30 December:

Mr C had taken some excellent photographs of the model and it was decided that as prints could be made in forty-eight hours if needed urgently there was no immediate need for them. Mr L reported Councillor C's request that the model might be shown to the Conservative members of the Borough Council, but this was thought to be most inadvisable. The model can be seen by all Councillors of all parties on January 3 when it goes to the Civic Centre . . . for further study by the Planning Committee.

Action Committee minutes, 11 March 1966:

Treasurer's Report. . . . Fighting Fund stands at £746 and 250 guineas have been paid by the Treasurer to Mr Napley. It was reported that an officer of the GLC had suggested that the Borough Council might relax somewhat and soft-pedal the Town Plan, as nothing whatever could happen until fifteen years hence, as the financial situation would influence the position. . . . Letters from Lords Euston and Esher were read and it was decided to take Lord Esher's advice and contact the Fine Arts Commission about the Town Plan and the alternative plan with a view to asking their help at the enquiry.

Action Committee minutes, 14 April 1966:

Important to find out exactly when the GLC have made their formal observations on the Town Plan to the Borough Council.

Action Committee minutes, 9 May 1966:

The compromise plan put up by the Borough Council was discussed at some length. It was decided that Mr Napley should see the plan and realise how this new plan to extend

13 Magdalene College, Cambridge, after.

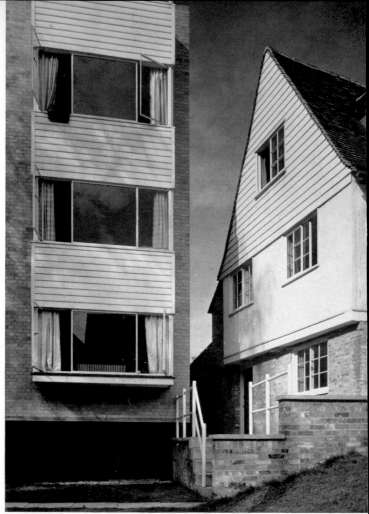

14 and 15
Magdalene
College,
Cambridge,
after.

the Civic Centre and house thousands of local government employees would add tremendously to the cost. . . Mr Napley should write to the Borough Council stating our views on this new plan and giving reasons for the Committee's dislike. . . . It was felt that though this new plan was an improvement on the original one, it does not remove our objections to the Town Plan. Referring to the 'depressed road' it was felt that this would be a preferable idea to the surface road if the enquiry goes against us.

Save Enfield Campaign to Mr W (a well-wisher), 19 July 1966:

It was kind of you to write and let me know of Ian Nairn's revived interest . . . As soon as we are told of the actual date of the public enquiry we must once more make a direct appeal to Ian Nairn for his support.

We are now in the throes of planning an intensive fund-raising drive as we feel the enquiry may well go on for some time . . . a gruesome thought.

Action Committee minutes, 13 July 1966:

A letter from Mr Napley was read. . . . He requested the Committee's permisison to show the Report to the Church solicitors with whom he has been in touch strictly confidentially. He has been informed that Rev D is very disturbed by the Council's plan for the church property, particularly the Vicarage garden. . . . It was emphasised that Mr Napley must guide the Committee in matters of finance but will he allow us to disclose anything in order to raise funds? . . . Dr R said the first step was to make sure that the public understood that the Town Plan is not any further forward except in the Borough Councillors' minds. . . . A great deal of discussion followed and during this it was agreed that the Committee should take credit for making the Council modify the original plan.

From The Observer Weekend Review, 24 July:

A Tale of Two Precincts, by Ian Nairn. The commuter line ends at Enfield Town and the station is well named; it is a true town. When you stand in the market place or sit out in Henekey's beer garden, London could be a hundred miles away, not because Enfield feels remote but through the town's own individuality. It depends on the way the square shades into the leafy churchyard, and from there into parks and narrow alleys. The countryside itself—really good stuff too, lush and hilly—is only a mile away. It is this relationship which is threatened by the fourth arm of a ring road of which three parts could be completed without damage. The original proposals attracted opposition to the tune of 12,000 signatures; now the Council propose sinking the road five feet.

But this will never do; it is a matter of intimate scale and silence and big bushes and intricate footpaths. One walk in the huge bosky churchyard is enough to prove that any road here is out of the question: the point is driven home by notices put up by the local opposition which say: 'This is where the proposed ring road would run. If you wish to preserve these quiet walks, get in touch with. . . . There can be no better way of showing awful consequences before they actualy happen: every local society ought to use this weapon and I think every council or developer ought to be compelled by law to state its intentions in this way on the ground.

Draft Notice of Objection
In the Matter of the Town and Country Planning Act 1962 and in the matter of the proposals, alterations and addition to the Middlesex Development Plan, Enfield Town Centre Comprehensive Development Area, and Objection No 28 thereto: As solicitors for and on behalf of the Save Enfield Campaign we hereby submit the following objections and representations in respect of the proposed alterations and additions to the County of Middlesex Development Plan as set out in the Written Statement and Report of Survey, and in the plans accompanying the said proposals (hereinafter called 'the Proposals';—[1] Enfield town centre—and more particularly the northern portion thereof—provides an area, unusual in close proximity to London, which has retained the atmosphere of a country town with historical associations. Whilst the need for some measure of redevelopment is indicated . . . . Kingsley, Napley and Company, Solicitors for an on behalf of the objectors.

Action Committee minutes, 5 August 1966:

Report on meeting with Mr Napley. . . . The public enquiry may be in February or March 1967, three months' notice will be given to the Committee. Mr Napley advised that £2,000 may be needed for the opposition if the enquiry goes on for three weeks. This will mean he will have to concentrate on the enquiry and put all other work aside.

It was decided that we must raise as much money as we can, but as soon as the date is known, then go to Mr Napley and tell him exactly how much we have in the Fighting Fund.

Mr Napley informed the members present that he had decided not to use the model at the enquiry as the basis of our opposition. He felt the financial situation of the country had put a different aspect on the entire position and we should press for a concentrated effort to speed traffic in Enfield and for the building of the D ring road.[1] This would cope with the situation for the next few years and will give all parties time to evaluate the position. He felt it was a better plan to convince the Ministry this way . . . He advised the Committee not to use the model in the fund-rasing meetings planned for the autumn. He reminded the members that if we stand by the alternative plan people who are not in agreement with it will withdraw their support at the enquiry. This is the danger.

He would like to fight at the enquiry on nearly all the points raised by Ian Nairn in his 'Observer' article. He felt it was up to the Council to provide a traffic solution in Enfield without any destruction of buildings and he advised the Committee to work on this line. . . . He is very much against the large public meeting to gain support and funds when the date of enquiry is known. He feels that the Council are banking on his using the alternative plan at the enquiry and by not doing so they will be foxed. His aim is to urge the Inspector to report to the Minister that nothing needs to be done in Enfield and this will line up with all the economies at present. The country's financial

[1] This was the outermost of the four ring roads then being proposed by the GLC.

troubles will last for a long period. . . . A discussion on the foregoing points then followed, chiefly on how to raise essential funds without the model being the focal point of the proposed meetings. . . . It was felt that we cannot hold the seventh conference without showing our supporters the model. The difficulty will be to wake up the audience without some similar attraction.

Action Committee minutes, 1 September 1966:

As Mr Napley is not to use the model of the alternative plan at the enquiry, we are set back eighteen months in our work. . . . The Secretary suggested every buyer of the reprint of Whittaker's "History of Enfield" produced last year by the Enfield Preservation Society, should be approached for a donation to the Fighting Fund. This was decided upon.'

Action Committee minutes, 28 October 1966:

The Chairman reported that he had seen Mr Pullen and he has promised to be available to help at the public enquiry. It is hoped to confine Mr Pullen's attendance to two days so to limit the costs. The Chairman felt that it will be essential to say frankly to both Mr Pullen and Mr Napley, before the enquiry, how much money the Committee can spend, and then arrangements can be made accordingly. It was thought Mr Pullen might charge at least £100 odd. It was emphasised that his presence at the enquiry was very important. . . . The Chairman said he hoped to speak to the Enfield Rotary Club on the work and hopes of the Campaign, soft-pedalling Mr Napley's plans for the enquiry. It is hoped to encourage the Rotarians to give great big donations to the Fighting Fund.

Letter from Mr Pullen to the Chairman of the Save Enfield Campaign:

I confirm that I shall be available to give evidence at a public enquiry on behalf of your society. The fees will be 100 guineas plus out of pocket expenses, and 30 guineas for each additional day after the first.

Action Committee minutes, 13 January 1967:

Fighting Fund: £641.

Action Committee minutes, 17 February 1967:

Stall holders and husbands to meet on Friday, March 10 at 19 Gentleman's Row for sherry and discussion. The members of the Action Committee agreed to share the cost of the sherry. . . . June flower arrangement meeting in June.

Action Committee minutes, 30 March 1967:

Tombola prizes were then discussed and it was decided that as many prizes as possible should be obtained from all sources. The Secretary promised to round up some young people to help run it.

Action Committee minutes, 28 April 1967:

Mr G had given permission for the Tudor Room for the floral lunch on June 21.

About this time officials in the Ministry of Housing and Local Government began to discuss an unusual initiative: namely whether they should recommend the Minister responsible to reject the road plan without waiting for the public enquiry. Ian Nairn's article had had its effect on them, too. They realised that in order to create a pedestrian shopping area, the proposed new ring road would destroy an existing pedestrian 'precinct' of probably greater charm than anything that even the Borough of Enfield in their wisdom could create. They remembered that, before it vanished from the scene, the County Planning Authority of Middlesex had disliked the scheme, that some of the officers of the Borough of Enfield itself still disliked it, and that the Greater London Council Planning Committee would not have submitted it to the Minister at all if they had had the courage to stand up to their more forceful colleagues on the Highways side. Nor could it be argued that the traffic problem of Enfield was insoluble by any other means.

So, after some diligent walking round, the officials
concerned recommended to their superiors that sooner
than involve everyone in the protracted horrors of a
public local enquiry, the honest thing to do would be
to reject the proposal there and then. Their seniors
agreed that the plan should be thrown back at the local
authority without a local enquiry. This would be a
drastic but not unprecedented action, and it seemed
wrong that a large number of people should be subjected
to the trouble and the expense of a public enquiry into
something which everybody at the Ministry believed to
be fundamentally unsound, and which in any case came
very low in the capital investment list.

The responsible junior ministers, who were at that
time Mr James McColl and the present writer, agreed.

*Ministry of Housing and Local Government to Greater
London Council, 10 May 1967:*

I am directed by the Minister of Housing and Local
Government to refer to the proposals now before him for
defining some fifty-five acres of land in the centre of Enfield
as an area of comprehensive development. . . . The Minister's principal objection to the scheme is that the northern
arm of the road would destroy the present form of the
churchyard and the system of footpaths surrounding the
church which make so great a contribution to the distinctive
character of Enfield. He notes that it is the present intention to sink the road where it runs through the churchyard
but this could at best only mitigate the disruptive effect
on the present amenities of this part of the town.

The Minister has concluded that the certain effects of
the prospects on the church and its surroundings outweigh
the possibility of benefit likely to be gained from the scheme.
. . . Accordingly the Minister rejects the proposals submitted
to him for the amendment of the development plan. . . .
The Minister does not wish to take up a purely negative
attitude. He therefore thinks he should indicate points for
consideration which may be helpful in preparing any fresh
proposals for implementation in the future. . . . Bearing

in mind the need to restrict the demand on capital investment. . . . the Minister suggests that in considering any
future proposals the local planning authority should bear in
mind the need for preserving and enhancing the present
character of Enfield and particularly the area north of
Church Street. They should consider how far loading and
unloading difficulties can be countered by traffic management as distinct from the creation of new roads, and what
is the shortest length of new road necessary to achieve an
acceptable traffic solution.

Secretary of the Save Enfield Campaign to Mr Pullen,
16 May:

My Committee have asked me to send you the wonderful
news that the Minister, Mr Greenwood, has turned down
the Council's Town Plan without having the public enquiry
we have been working so hard for. Perhaps you heard this
on the news last Friday. We are so very grateful for all
you have done to help us and we hope that you will be
able to be present at the Preservation Society dinner later
in the year which we would like to call the Celebration
Dinner! More about that later.

Action Committee, 19 May:

All the letters of thanks to helpers at the spring market
have been sent off immediately after the market day. . . .
It was decided that as there was now no need for a public
enquiry after all, it was no longer an urgency to organise
the proposed floral luncheon. This was cancelled forthwith.

Treasurer's Report: £1,024. A letter from Mr Napley was
read congratulating the Committee. The final account of Mr
Napley would be sent shortly . . . Moved . . . that 'When
balance is known it should be invested in the Enfield Building Society inviting the Enfield Preservation Society to be
the holding trustees. The Action Committee to review the
situation at least once a year.' Seconded and carried unanimously. . . . Final conference. It was decided after some discussion that there is no need for this . . . Mr F moved that
the sum of £10 be paid to the Honorary Secretary for all
telephone calls since 1961. This was carried. The Hon Secretary put forward the idea of a Board commemorating the

success of the Campaign to be put up in the churchyard.
There was no enthusiasm for this idea and it was dropped.

MOTCOMB STREET,
WESTMINSTER

Motcomb Street is a minor tributary of Belgravia, and
Belgravia is, after the ·Nash Terraces round Regents
Park, the grandest scheme ever made of early nineteenth
century English urban housing. It is the archetype of the
combination of square with mews and terrace with mews
which arose from, conditioned, and in the end prolonged
the class structure of nineteenth century capitalism. The
working classes who used to be servants of the rich
people have attained independence and moved elsewhere. The rich people have moved into their former
houses in the mews, and Embassies and offices have
moved in turn into the rich peoples' houses in front.

Motcomb Street is a thoroughly pleasing little street
with shops, and two eccentric Grecian buildings full of
panache, facing each other: 'the Pantechnicons'. In the
early 1960s a developer began to cast envious eyes on
this very lucrative site, between Belgravia and Knights-
bridge, and, since it was not actually Belgrave Square
itself, thought he stood a chance. Supported by the
ground landlord, he applied for planning permission to
demolish the whole street and the little bits round the
corners out of it, including both Pantechnicons, and to
put up a standard tower and podium block. The Greater
London Council countered by refusing permission and
placing a building preservation order[1] on thirty-four of
the properties concerned, including the Pantechnicons.
The developer and landlord appealed.

The lie of the land can be seen from the map at page
186 and the present appearance of Motcomb Street, after

[1]See p. 76.

the happy ending to be described below, can be seen from the photograph at plate 10.

From the report of Mr C, one of the Minister's Inspectors, to the Minister of Housing and Local Government, 7 January 1966:

Sir, I have the honour to report that on Tuesday 19 October 1965 I opened a join enquiry into. . . .

The reasons for the GLC's refusal of the appeal were as follows:

The proposal does not comply with the Council's plot-ratio standards. The proposal would provide for offices, which is contrary to the intention of the County of London development plan, in which the area is primarily allocated for residential purposes with a shopping frontage to Motcomb Street, and would also result in an increase in office floor space which is contrary to the Council's policy to resist proposals which would increase congestion in the central part of London by substantially raising the office potential on the site, with a consequent further burden on the already overloaded public transport facilities.

The proposal does not comply with the Council's daylighting standard. . . .

The lay-out and massing indicated in the scheme fails to preserve the scale of development which characterises the area. . . .

The siting of the petrol filling station . . . is unsatisfactory as it would seriously detract from the amenities of adjoining residential properties. Furthermore, the location of the petrol filling station is objectionable on traffic grounds . . .

The Buildings, the Appeal Site and Surroundings
The buildings consist of narrow and mainly stucco fronted houses three and four storeys high including basements with shops on the ground floor, together with two large buildings of monumental character, also stucco fronted, the Pantechnicons, standing opposite to each other near the south west end of Motcomb Street. All were built between 1825 and 1841 and all the houses had shops by 1845, some having been designed with shops originally.

The Pantechnicon on the north west side of the street, still known by that name, . . . is three storeys high with a row of giant Greek Doric engaged columns supporting an entablature and a blind attic storey. The building was designed primarily for the display, sale and storage of carriages and is now used as auction galleries and for furniture storage.

The other Pantechnicon, referred to as Trollope's Warehouse, is a three storey building extending through to West Halkin Street. . . . It was designed mainly as shops and show rooms, including two shopping arcades linking the two streets . . . The most recent use of this building was as display galleries and warehousing . . . and also as offices, but it is now being restored to its original use, including the shopping arcades.

The Order Buildings on the appeal site have been . . . found to contain a number of defects due to their age, . . . the important ones being worn out and leaking roofs, sagging floors and damp basements generally, some dry rot . . . bulging walls . . . and badly cracked basement arches. The defects generally were not contested by either Council (i.e. the GLC or Westminster City Council) and were evident during my inspection.

The case for the Greater London Council and the Westminster City Council relating to the preservation order.

The former London County Council considered that both sides of Motcomb Street, together with the other buildings in the Order in Lowndes Street and West Halkin Street, were worthy of preservation and resolved to make the order . . . in 1965. The development of Belgravia, the crowning achievement of the great contractor Thomas Cubitt, 1788-1855, came about as the result of the transformation of Buckingham House from 1821 onwards into a royal palace . . . In 1825 Seth-Smith covenanted with the Grosvenor Estate to develop about seventeen acres leased from the Estate on the north-western end of the Belgravia area . . . In December 1823, Seth-Smith asked for permission to abandon the sewer in Gresford Street and to build instead a sewer in West Halkin Street to connect with a proposed new sewer to be built by Thomas Cubitt . . . The revision of the lay-out gave Seth-Smith additional frontages to Motcomb Street and West Halkin Street within the Grosvenor Estate, and he built on

these, in 1830-31, his two buildings of monumental character described collectively in his original prospectus as The
Pantechnicon and bearing that name on their façades . . .
The architect was probably Joseph Jopling . . . The houses
in this corner of Belgravia were intended for the trades
people who supplied the needs of the wealthy residents . . .

The appreciation of the architectural style and quality of
building is subject in a high degree to changes of fashion
and taste, and other important elements of architectural
interest have also to be considered before deciding whether
that interest is 'special'.[1] These elements are (1) rarity; (2)
integrity in the sense of freedom from greater alteration;
and (3) public appreciation.

The buildings covered by the Order pass all these tests.
Their merits under the three headings as follows:—

Rarity
The two Pantechnicons are undoubtedly unique buildings
in regard to both their design and purpose. The other
buildings are admittedly typical of the sort of buildings
being erected generally at the time, but scarcity is coming
to the fore as more and more redevelopment takes place.
The design of Motcomb Street as a domestic street with the
two monumental buildings opposite each other is itself a
rarity.

Integrity
All the listed buildings, supplementary as well as statutory,
are virtually unaltered externally . . .

Public appreciation
The evidence as to this is considerable. To start with the
Order was made not by experts but by the elected representatives of London as a whole with the support of the elected
representatives of the more local Westminster City Council;
and since then has been added the support of the following
public bodies:— Georgian Group, Victorian Society, Westminster Society, London Society, and London and Middlesex
Archaeological Society. There is a petition with some 400
signatures submitted at this enquiry in support of the Order.

[1]The word in the 1962 Act.

Conclusion
All the buildings have distinct merits. The two pantechnicons are striking examples of late Regency work and the whole group, whose survival is both fortunate and surprising, makes the most attractive and historically the most valuable composition of contrasting types of buildings of their period ranging from the monumental to the domestic. . . . The value of this group of buildings is enhanced by its position leading to one of the monuments of the period in London, Belgrave Square . . . If the Minister should regrettably acquiesce in the destruction of the north-west side of Motcomb Street as intended by the appellants, then the integrity of the street as an example of its period would be lost and there would be little point in retaining the south-east side by itself. It is in fact a case of all or nothing . . .

Legal Submissions
Submission on behalf of the Westminster City Council. The Order requires amending at the top of page five to make it clear that the authority upon whom a purchase notice must be served is the Westminster City Council.[1]
Submission on behalf of the Greater London Council.
There is no doubt that the Order as it now stands must be amended so as to state the identity of the authority upon whom purchase notices must be served, and it is maintained that the authority should properly be the Greater London Council.

The case for Capital and Counties Property Company Limited, the appellants, and the Grosvenor Estate.
. . . The appellants are the freeholders of numbers 20-23 Motcomb Street and 15-21 Lowndes Street, and building lessees for the whole of the remainder by virtue of a ninety-nine year lease granted by the Grosvenor Estate in December 1963 . . . The development of Belgravia was carried out as a speculation between 1825 and 1835 in an area of grand and formalised town planning in fairly good, if slightly debased, classical detail . . .

---

[1] That is if, after the confirmation of the Order, the owner were able to prove that he had been deprived of reasonable beneficial use of his property. See p. 78.

Belgravia also included a number of quite pleasant lesser streets, of which Motcomb Street is one, fitted in rather awkwardly behind the big squares . . . Belgravia never bore the hallmark of refinement and elegance belonging to the Regency and the work of Nash, but in its great days of the Victorian and Edwardian era, with its building development as a whole freshly painted every year in time for the season, it undoubtedly formed a single architectural entity.

While this is still true of the 'central citadel' of Belgravia . . . which remains virtually intact, the situation is very different on the fringes and in the hinterland as the result of erosion with new buildings of different type and the gradual mutilation of less important back streets such as Motcomb Street.

In the area west of Belgrave Square in particular there is the unfortunate dull neo-Georgian brickwork in Lowndes Square, allowed before the War, and since the War many other new buildings have been erected, such as the Carlton Tower Hotel in Cadogan Place, Lowndes Court and Bolebec House in Lowndes Street, and the telephone exchange in Chesham Place.

This situation demands a new policy in Belgravia on the part of the Greater London Council. Instead of trying to preserve odd listed buildings as and when threatened anywhere, they should adopt a policy of encouraging the inevitable new development in response to social change in the mutilated hinterland, and at the same time firmly preserve the 'central citadel' which should be precisely defined in area and declared absolutely inviolate. Such a policy would be both realistic towards the present and civilised towards the past.

Motcomb Street is a short, mutilated street in the hinterland, lined mainly with small terrace houses . . . Suffered alterations . . . More or less incongruous shop fronts added . . . Monumental and totally out of scale Pantechnicon . . . The use of a giant order in the confined space of Motcomb Street is wholly inappropriate, and would never have been contemplated by Nash or the Woods of Bath, who only used it when it could be seen across an open space in a setting of the right scale . . . The Pantechnicon is in fact thoroughly bad aesthetically, as a piece of three-dimensional town planning, as well as bad functionally as a modern warehouse, and its only possible claim to distinction must lie in its proportion and purity of detail as a connoisseur's specimen.

In this respect as an essay in the use of the Greek doric order, derived presumably from the Parthenon, the essence of which is purity and corectitude, the Pantechnicon fails to make the grade on a number of counts. For example: (1) The slender proportion of the columns — six and a half diameters high compared with the Parthenon's five and a half—accentuated by their separate pedestals instead of the Pathenon's continuous stylobate or platform, and resulting in a loss of the sturdy robustness characteristic of Greek doric. (2) The variation of the inter-columniation to provide wider bays for the two entrances, an inevitable result of trying to reproduce a design to half its size. (3) The use of arches over the entrances, which is an architectural solecism when introduced into a design based on the pure trabeated style of Greek doric . . . Whilst it may once have been an integral part of the fine Belgravia conception, it is so no longer, but is rather an integral part of the jumble of old property extending northwards . . .

Conclusion
The buildings generally in Motcomb Street, and in particular those on its north-west side, have little intrinsic merit architecturally. The area generally north west of this street is ripe for redevelopment, and the free form of redevelopment now proposed for the appeal site in the modern idiom of podium and tower blocks is entirely appropriate in this position, where it would in no way damage or threaten Belgrave Square or any other part of 'the central citadel' of Belgravia deemed worthy of preservation.

The Case for the Westminster City Council opposing the appeal
. . . The London County Council consulted various public bodies . . . The Commissioner of Police and the Ministries of Transport and Works raised no objection to the scheme. The Ministry of Housing and Local Government said that the demolition of a listed building would be regrettable.

The Royal Fine Arts Commission considered that any re-development scheme should retain the façade of the Pantechnicon and preserve more of the scale and character of the area . . . Out of 150 adjoining owners and occupiers notified by the London County Council of the proposed scheme, twenty-three replied. Of these, three raised no objection and the objections of the others included the loss of architectural character and interference with the amenities of the locality, . . . loss of view, overshadowing, overlooking and the re-siting of the existing filling station and garage.

Conclusion
It is considered that the appeal should be dismissed because (1) the proposal means the destruction of buildings which ought to be preserved and (2) even if these buildings cannot after all be saved, the proposed new development . . . is (1) utterly alien in character to the Belgravian scene; (2) an overdevelopment of the site with an excessive amount of non-residential uses.

The case for other interested persons
Mr Fello-Atkinson for the Georgian Group: The Group have been worried for a considerable time about the fate of the Pantechnicon and are of the opinion that preservation of the whole group of buildings covered by the Order is essential. The loss of any of the buildings now threatened would be very regrettable as being the first step towards destroying the homogeneity of the Belgravia area as a whole, and the Preservation Order is strongly supported.

The Westminster Society are in full agreement with the statement made on behalf of the Georgian Group.

Miss M, as an inhabitant of this area living at her present address for the last twenty-one years, supports the Order . . .

Major-General Sir Drummond English, KBE, CBE, MC, Baileys Printers Ltd, Falcon Street, Ipswich. He was until quite recently the owner of a lease on No 17 Motcomb Street as partner in a firm carrying on a business there. The condition of the building was thoroughly bad in all respects, including the antique plumbing and electric wiring . . . The Pantechnicon is a monstrosity . . . The Preservation Order is an example of the dead hand of officialdom, and the

Minister is urged to reject the Order so that the street can be redeveloped.

The GLC's 'Reasons for Refusal'
With the single exception of Sir Drummond English, the former owner of 17 Motcomb Street, with his views about officialdom and the 'monstrous' character of the Pantechnicon, the opposition to the Order is restricted to the evidence of Professor Furneaux Jordan.

The Professor's views are entitled to the greatest respect, but are of a highly personal nature, reflecting an apparent lack of sympathy with the Belgravian type of architecture. He accepts the need for some preservation in Belgravia but would limit it to the principal squares and streets described by him as the 'central citadel', and then as examples of fine town planning rather than fine architectural quality.

He disapproves of the Pantechnicon because it disregards the rules for the use of the Greek doric order exemplified in the Parthenon. But it is useless to criticise a building designed as a warehouse in the early nineteenth century, using free classical form in the manner prevalent at that time, for not obeying the precise rules considered suitable for a Greek temple in the fifth century BC. That sort of criticism does nothing to denigrate the Pantechnicon's special architectural interest.

The Council also contests the Professor's view that homogeneity in the street scene cannot be achieved in a small street like Motcomb Street without architectural uniformity. They maintain that homogeneity has resulted in this case from the carrying out of all the development within about fifteen years, with the two monumental buildings harmonising with the rest generally in height, materials and classical style.

Once it is decided that the buildings are worthy of preservation as examples of their period, it is idle to complain that they are old and worn, and some degree of maintenance problem is inevitable . . . Their defects are generally such as one would expect to find in buildings of their age.

With regard to expediency, there is clearly no problem of finding continuing uses for the buildings, except possibly the Pantechnicons.

Inspector's Conclusions

It is fair to describe the buildings as a whole covered by the Order as possessing special architectural or historic interest. But that does not mean that all should necessarily be preserved, as they are not properly part of the central system of squares and streets described by Professor Jordan as the central citadel of Belgravia which it would be desirable to preserve intact, and it would be unreasonable to preserve the whole of Belgravia. . . . I am inclined to the view that the preservation of the north-west side of Motcomb Street would not be justified in view of (a) the generally poor condition of the buildings internally; (b) the likely difficulty in making use of the shallow depth of the Pantechnicon covered by the Order; (c) the improvements in the area made possible by the scheme under appeal in regard to lay-out, living standards, possibly also traffic conditions; and (d) the fact that replacement with development in the modern idiom of podium and tower would leave Belgrave Square unaffected.

The Order is justified in respect to the remaining group of buildings south-east of Motcomb Street both by their architectural quality and by the position of this group where it is seen from Belgrave Square.

Preservation of this side of Motcomb Street is not invalidated by the loss of the north-west side . . . There are valid objections to the scheme as submitted in regard to the office accommodation, the filling station and garage and various daylighting infringements.

There is no objection in principle to development on the lines of the amended scheme subject to the exclusion of the filling station and garage.

There is no objection to the inclusion of petrol filling facilities provided that they are limited to the use of residents on and visitors to the site . . .

Ninety feet above pavement level should be the maximum height for any part of the new development, so as to protect Belgrave Square.

Inspector's Recommendations

(A) I recommend that :

1   In respect of all the buildings to the south-east of Motcomb Street the Order be confirmed . . .

2   In respect of all the buildings to the north-west of
Motcomb Street the Order be not confirmed.

(B) **The appeal** : I recommend that the appeal be dismissed,
but without prejudice to the submission of a fresh application. . . .'

The Inspector's report was received with some reserve
in the Ministry. The geographical planning branch for
London took the initiative, with the support of the
Historic Buildings Branch (which was not at that time
as strong as it later became), in recommending that the
Minister should not accept the Inspector's report. It was
their view that the destruction of Motcomb Street as an
entity would be an irreparable loss to the London scene,
and that was a matter of general planning concern. They
did not find the arguments which the Inspector accepted
in favour of new development at all convincing. Among
the reasons against preservation, the Inspector had mentioned that the replacement of Motcomb Street in the
modern idiom of podium and tower would leave
Belgrave Square unaffected. This was where he had
fallen into error. The Greater London Council and the
City of Westminster had each separately argued the
case for preservation on at least three grounds (a) the
merits of individual buildings; (b) the value of Motcomb
Street as a group of buildings; and (c) the relationship
of Motcomb Street to Belgrave Square. Professor
Furneaux Jordan, who gave evidence on behalf of the
developers, had argued that only the 'central citadel of
Belgravia' was worth preserving, and Motcomb Street
was not an integral part of the central citadel. In his
conclusions, the Inspector seemed to have given weight
only to argument (c) above, and on Professor Jordan's
evidence he rejected it. He had given inadequate weight
to the Belgrave Square argument, and no weight at all to
the merit of Motcomb Street itself. It would be wrong to

accept that only the 'central citadel of Belgravia' was worth preserving, and that if Motcomb Street did not contribute to Belgrave Square it could therefore be demolished, even though it had merit as an entity in itself. If it were decided to disagree with the Inspector a decision paragraph could be produced which accepted his facts but disagreed with his conclusions on the grounds that he had not given adequate weight to the various aspects of the case for preservation as put by the planning authorities. Westminster and the GLC each wanted to be named in the Building Preservation Order as the acquiring authority, should a Purchase Notice be served. It would be best to encourage Westminster (who were showing considerable initiative and quality in civic design) by naming them rather than the GLC, who would have their hands full elsewhere.

So far as the appeal was concerned, this must in any case be dismissed because the appeal proposals included offices. But the applicants had produced alternative proposals during the enquiry with flats instead of offices, and the Inspector would accept this if a filling station were re-sited. But any new development should retain the scale of development which already prevailed; otherwise there might be an attempt to crowd everything on to the remainder of the appeal site (i.e. the rest of the Lowndes Street frontage and the south-western side of Kinnerton Street). A general statement should safeguard the position at any rate until the local planning authority had an opportunity to consider action under the Civic Amenities Bill when it became law.

The senior officials concerned agreed that this was the sort of unpretentiously pleasant area which is part of the charm of London, and that it was a much better foil to the 'central citadel' of Belgravia than the stock central-area-type scheme offered by the developers. 'Improved traffic conditions' would not be a benefit in a place like this, but a menace to an 'environmental area'.

The junior minister concerned, then the present

writer, accepted the official advice. I even went a little further and thought that the Inspector's opinion that 'it would be unreasonable to preserve the whole of Belgravia' suggested that some of the Inspectorate were out of touch with current thought and policy. I asked if the Inspectors ever met together, so that there could be a general discussion of preservation policy. (They did, and there was.)

Ministry of Housing to Messrs Debenham & Co, Solicitors, London, 29 September 1966:
'I am directed by the Minister of Housing and Local Government to say that he has considered the report of his Inspector into (a) the appeal of your clients, Capital and Counties Property Co Ltd against the decision of the London County Council to refuse planning permission . . . (b) an application by the Greater London Council for the confirmation of a Building Preservation Order . . . The Minister accepts the Inspector's findings of fact and notes his conclusions. He agrees that there are valid objections to the scheme as submitted in regard to the filling station and garage, and various daylighting infringements. Accordingly he accepts the Inspector's recommendation that he should dismiss the appeal, which he hereby does . . . So far as the Building Preservation Order is concerned the Minister agrees with the Inspector's conclusion that the buildings as a whole covered by the Order deserve special architectural or historic interest. He considers that, in concluding that the Order for the buildings on the north-west side of Motcomb Street should not be confirmed, the Inspector has not given adequate weight to the arguments for preservation put forward by the planning authorities and interested persons. In particular he does not think the Inspector has attached sufficient importance to the architectural and historic merits of the individual buildings, and to their importance as a group in the street scene. Nor does he accept that the preservation of buildings in Belgravia should necessarily be limited to those in what the report describes as the "central citadel" of Belgravia. He has accordingly decided to confirm the Building Preservation Order in respect of all the buildings named in it.'

The Northern Pantechnicon has now been restored by Sothebys as an auction room for Victoriana.

CONCLUSION

This final section has set out four stories; four fairly detailed accounts of struggles, all but one successful, to save or restore some part of the amenity of England.

The first, Beaufort Square in Bath, was the story of how the reconstruction of part and the preservation of the whole of a little square was achieved over five years without a ministerial enquiry or decision and without any expenditure at all, by a persevering and resourceful local society. This Stukeley is an object lesson in the knight's move, which is the essence of all practical politics.

The second, the story of The Hall, an old house in Gosport, showed a sudden last minute attempt by a boy of sixteen to prevent an unauthorised demolition by a philistine town council. He had his history and his law right; local and national press and local television leaped to befriend him, but he was too late, and the building was lost. He should have started before he was born, and built up a local amenity society.

The third, the Enfield Road, was the story of how a pleasant place was saved from a juggernaut and superfluous road by a specially created local campaign, grouping twenty-six pre-existent organisations, working arduously over seven years for money to pay for professional help at a ministerial enquiry. It was a Lubbock. In the end the road proposal was turned down by the Government without an enquiry, but it would not have been if there had not been such clear evidence of local opposition.

The fourth, Motcomb Street in Westminster, showed a set-piece legal battle before a minister's inspector with all the traditional cast acting to the top of their bent.

The big property developer casts envious eyes on a plum
site in the centre of a rich city. He brings eccentric and
purist professional evidence to prove that the buildings
now on the site are not as good as the Parthenon. All the
relevant national amenity societies protest to high heaven
the thing must not be done. Two major local authorities,
London and Westminster, agree; not much in London is
as good as the Parthenon they say, but London is yet
worth keeping. The Inspector wavers; while it would
be wrong to sacrifice all, yet it would be equally wrong
not to sacrifice any. Perhaps a Solomon solution. In the
end the Government backs the elected local councillors,
and preserves.

It would be possible without repetition to tell many
more stories in detail, so wide is the experience of the
amenity movement, and so many ways are there of going
about it. But what remains to be said can now be said
in a shorter and more general way.

The most successful Aubrey yet practised must be the
Plymouth Barbican scheme (and we have not yet discussed an Aubrey). It may indeed be the largest and
boldest preservation scheme ever carried out in this
country by a private, property-owning trust mainly
reliant on public subscription.

The 'Barbican' is in fact the old town of Plymouth,
round the harbour of Sutton Pool, and running up to
the castle. In 1957 the City Council wanted to knock
down fifty-six houses there, to begin with, and to rebuild
with four-storey blocks of flats in order to get the housing
subsidy which was then payable on buildings of that
height and above. There was a battle royal in the local
press, in which the issue was largely determined by the
copious and scholarly articles of Mr Crispin Gill, the
deputy editor of the *Western Morning News*, who wrote
anonymously.[1] The City Council also divided sharply,

[1] He has also written a useful pamphlet, ' *Plymouth Barbican
Revived*', obtainable from the Plymouth Barbican Association
Ltd, 70 Mutley Plain, Plymouth.

and both parties were split. There was already an Old Plymouth Society, and this body hived off a non profit making trust, the Plymouth Barbican Association Ltd, which succeeded in getting 999-year leases from the City Council on nine houses in the Barbican and buying the freehold of thirteen more.

The operations of the Association have been more practical than is always the case with preservationist groups, and this is largely due to the prominence in it of a chartered accountant, Mr Stanley Edgcumbe. The income of the Association over the first twelve years of its existence has been as follows:

Rents	£14,000
Grants from central government	£6,600
Gifts and donations under covenant	£5,600
Pilgrim Trust	£2,000

The City Council were only dissuaded from bull-dozing everything and persuaded to issue leases to the Association by an undertaking that no families should remain in the Barbican (except in such new blocks of flats as might be built). Most of it had for many years been declared unfit for human habitation, and thus classified as a slum. The properties restored by the Association are therefore confined to uses other than domestic: a social club, offices and showrooms, an antique furniture dealer, a pottery studio, architects offices, etc. Even the Plymouth Chamber of Commerce has its office in the Barbican.

Dotted about the old streets there are a number of distinctive gin warehouses in which Plymouth gin lies under customs bond. These are fine rough limestone buildings of the seventeenth and eighteenth centuries, and the old houses ranging in date from Elizabethan to mid-nineteenth century string out prettily among them.

It has to be admitted that the Plymouth Barbican does now convey a feeling of unreality, almost of wilfulness. This is not the Association's fault: it is simply because nobody lives in the old houses, and it would disappear at once as soon as a few families were allowed to move back in. The Association intends to approach the Council shortly to seek the removal of the 'no dwellings' condition on which they were granted the leases. Since the condition was imposed in the late fifties, much has been learned about how to make old houses sanitary and habitable. If the empty upper storeys could be properly lived in again and there were a few children running around, the place would be really pleasant. Plate 10 gives an idea.

If that is the most successful Aubrey, the history of the York Civic Trust for the last twenty-five years is one of continuously successful Aubrey-Stukeley. It is the local society which, of all in England, has probably achieved the greatest mastery of this gambit. Time and again they have raised half the money necessary to preserve an old building or group and have then turned to the owners, as often as not the City Council, and assumed with a friendly smile that the owners would naturally wish to pay the other half. It almost always works. Dotted all over the city now are the pleasant and tidy jobs the York Civic Trust has done, each with a little plaque to say so. And each is a monument not only to the architecture of our forefathers, but also to the good temper of our own contemporary preservationists. It was not always so, but the York Civic Trust are now very much in Phase III, as I defined that in the third chapter of this book.

If, as is clearly the case, there is nothing like ownership for preserving old buildings, then voluntary societies can well learn from the techniques used by bodies which already own the buildings concerned. The restorations carried out by the Crown Estates to the great Nash terraces round Regents Park in London are the most heroic example of our days. For many years after the Second World War the Commissioners hesitated, and even from time to time advanced some disgraceful plans for demolition and redevelopment. But they were caught short by public opinion; for the last ten years they have been facing in the right direction, and have now even been persuaded to rebuild the bombed and patched up Cambridge Terrace. So now, (one by one), the cheap backstage brick of Nash's construction is scraped away and rebuilt behind those great gleaming facades, and one of the lightest and most cheerfully theatrical of palatial townscapes is safe for another century or so.

But this is preservation on a giant scale, and unfortunately it may be a decade or two yet before local amenity societies are anywhere strong enough to take on jobs of this size.

So it is convenient in conclusion, to look for an example of restoration and conversion which, irrespective of ownership, is in itself the most perfectly successful, and thus most worthy of study by all those, whether housing societies, housing associations, universities, or local authorities, who have a similar problem on their hands. It should be an area as opposed to one or two houses, but it should not be so big an area as to cause alarm and despondency at the mere prospect. It must have had that mixture of uses, from shop and warehouse to scruffy bedroom, and that mixture of building styles, from corrugated iron and breeze-block extension to satisfying hipped roof and even noble timber framing, which is characteristic of the back-lands gubbins of our historic towns.

Such an area belongs to Magdalene College, Cambridge, and lies between Magdalene Street, Northampton Street, and the river Cam. In 1953 it consisted of what can be seen at plates 11 and 12. In the eighteen years since then Messrs David Roberts and Geoffrey Clarke, architects, have converted the lot to student lodgings. The plan on pp. 204-5 is a key to the cost table at Appendix 2. Plates 13, 14 and 15 show what it looks like now.

The whole job has a brilliantly crisp and toothsome look to it, and fits in admirably with some new college buildings nearby. But, and here is the point; it cost a great deal less than new construction. The table at the appendix shows that lodgings for about seventy students cost about £77,000.[1] That gives an average cost of £1,100 per student, including 10% fees. During the years in question the rough cost of new built students' lodgings, financed by the University Grants Committee, was £1,600 per student, including $12\frac{1}{2}$% fees. It is true these costs are not strictly comparable; Magdalene College had its just-usable gubbins to start with, and new buildings only have earth. But all the same the figures are encouraging to those who think the two problems of decaying old towns, and a student population increasing at the speed of light, should be put together. Two problems do not often add up to one solution, but they sometimes do, and in this case, in some parts of the country, they could.

The future of local societies for the preservation of old towns and buildings will lie, as has their past, between the Aubrey, the Stukeley, and the Lubbock. The Aubrey must come more and come to predominate. There could well be a great expansion of the local, county, or regional historic buildings trusts, registered as housing associations and enjoying all the grants housing associations enjoy, as well as the normal preservation and conversion grants. Local authority participation should be as great as each individual local democracy is ready to undertake.

The Stukeley should in due course die out, as it becomes less and less needed. It consists of shaming people into doing what they ought, and one must hope that they will increasingly do what they ought without being shamed into it.

The Lubbock is here for keeps, since there will always be profiteers who operate up to the edge of what the law allows. The law must therefore only allow what society is prepared to see happen.

The next steps for government were discussed on pages 102-5. The next step for local societies should, I believe,

---

[1] I have ignored items (l), (o), and (p).

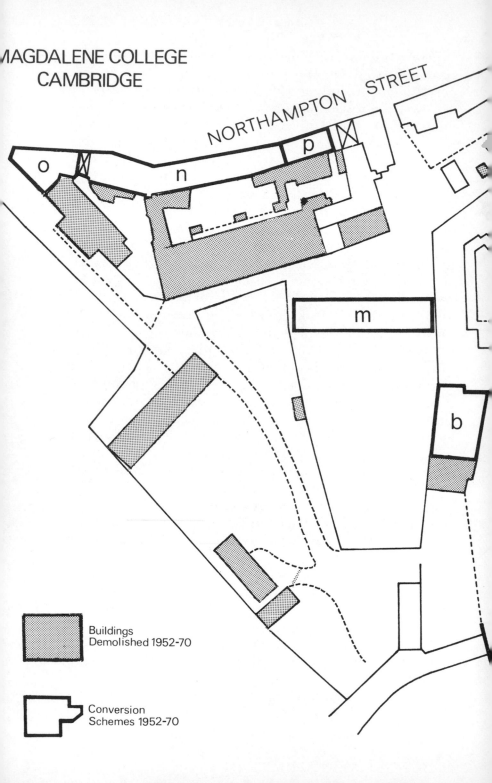

MAGDALENE COLLEGE
CAMBRIDGE

NORTHAMPTON STREET

o

n

p

m

b

Buildings
Demolished 1952-70

Conversion
Schemes 1952-70

tend more and more towards acquisition, and conversion, followed by resale, or leasing, or renting. This too, Government must favour, and it must realise that the main help it can give is money. The fact that the present government has taken the first step backwards in the history of preservation in this country is discussed on pages 98-9. It ought to be the last step backwards, as it was the first, and ought soon to be annulled and overtaken by intelligent and constructive advance.

Appendix I

The original instruction to the Investigators under the 1947 Act had read in its relevant passage:

'In Grade I should be placed buildings of such importance that their destruction should in no case be allowed; in Grade II, buildings whose preservation should be regarded as a matter of national interest so that though it may be that now and then the preservation of a Grade II building will have to give way before some other yet more important consideration of planning or the like, yet the Ministry will, in each case, take such steps that are in its power to avoid the necessity of this and where no conflict of national interest can be shown will take such positive steps as are open to it to secure the building's preservation. In Grade III will be placed: (1) Buildings of architectural or historic interest which do not, however, rise to the degree properly qualified as special; (2) Buildings which so contribute to a general effect that the planning authority ought, in the preparation and administration of its plans, to regard this effect as an asset worth trying to keep.'

The document in force at the time of the passage of the 1968 Act read as follows:

'The Statutory List comprises buildings grades I, II* and II. Legally there is no difference between these grades. They were intended to act as yard-sticks for measuring within the Ministry a building's importance, but they have come to have special significance outside as well as within the Ministry.

Grade I buildings are defined as buildings of such great architectural or historic interest that no public utility scheme of any kind ought to be allowed to interfere with them. Only just over 4,000 buildings have been listed in Grade I.

Grade II buildings are those of sufficient architectural or historic interest for their demolition not to be allowed without compelling reason. There are already over 100,000 buildings in this grade and will be many more. The star was therefore invented to single out the most distinguished in the grade which approximate to Grade I in importance. The number of buildings to which a star has been given has not been accurately assessed but probably does not exceed 10,000.

In assessing which buildings to include in the Statutory List, it is the practice to include all buildings of any significance dating from before about 1700 which survive substantially intact or which reveal from the outside their general form and outline, even though they may have undergone some alterations in the C18 or early C19, provided that these alterations do not take the form of mutilation. Such buildings may not be works of architecture in the same sense as the formal compositions of the C18, but they are examples of the history of architecture varying in importance according to their age and the number of their surviving ancient features. Any building which shows evidence of having been a C15 hallhouse, for instance, has unquestioned value. But the existence of early features of more primitive or archaeological nature, such as a cruck, can be sufficient grounds for considering a more minor building to be of statutory quality. Even in the case of the more numerous examples of timber-framed buildings which date from the late C16 and C17 presumption is for their inclusion, unless their whole character and outline have been overlaid in an unsightly manner.

For buildings dating from between about 1700 and about 1830-40 the practice is to include all those buildings of good quality which are substantially intact even though some of these may be quite modest buildings. After 1840 and until 1914 our instructions are to be increasingly selective and to include only the principal works of the principal architects, of whom a list of 25 has been drawn up by the Minister's Advisory Committee, and such other buildings as have a definite character and quality. In addition industrial archaeology is a new subject which has brought to the fore the claims of early industrial buildings that are either of

inherent architectural merit or of significance in the development of their own industry, whether nationally or locally.

When buildings stand in groups in towns and villages,
and the group, considered as a whole, is of sufficient importance for it to be desirable that every listable building in it
should receive statutory protection, it is justifiable to grade
every individual building in such a Group as II, even though
some of them, had they stood alone, would not qualify for
more than III.

In assessing the quality or significance of a building the
rarity or otherwise of a type of building in the particular
area in question must be taken into account, and indeed the
scarcity or otherwise of old or listable buildings in that
town or area should also be considered. In areas where
candidates for listing are scarce it is legitimate to evaluate
those that do exist slightly higher than would be the case in
areas where such buildings are numerous. But in certain
historic towns like Bath where the atmosphere of the town
rests on the fact that virtually the whole town centre is of
homogeneous or ancient character it is not sufficient for only
the finest examples of any period or style to be listed. Some
at least of the "tissue" of relatively less important but con-
necting buildings have considerable claim for statutory
listing. Most buildings are listed principally for their
exterior, as the Investgators have hitherto had no right of
access and therefore the interior is often an unknown
quantity which may enhance but cannot detract from the
merits of the exterior. But a building can be listed partly
or wholly for its interior such as medieval crypt, fine staircase, plastered ceiling, etc, if this is known to exist and to be
of sufficient quality.

The most obvious example of historic interest is a building which has an association with a named person or persons,
event or events, of national or local standing, (e.g. Disraeli's
house, Hughenden, Bucks; Mrs Gaskell's house in Man-
chester; Benjamin Franklin's house in Wardour Street).
Some of the buildings with historical associations may have
architectural interest as well. In cases where the building in
question has been altered since the date of the historic
associations in question, this of itself does not destroy the
historic interest provided that sufficient of the old building

survives to preserve the historical continuity, i.e. to be able to say that so and so's house is still in existence, however-much it has been altered or its features obscured. An example is Mrs Fitzherbert's house at Brighton of which the front elevation has been rebuilt and is even ugly, but much of the interior remains intact.

Historical interest can also extend to buildings of sociological significance which are part of local history (e.g. the former Banbury cake shop; the Bakewell pudding-shop; former schools, theatres, institutes, clubs or almshouses); or evidence of a vanished way of life (e.g. the village forge, lock-up, pound, poorhouse, or mill).

The Supplementary List of Grade III buildings comprises those buildings which might have been included in Grade II, had they been intact and unaltered, but have been so mutilated as hardly to justify statutory listing, or more modest buildings of less quality such as cottages or other buildings in the vernacular manner. Over 106,000 buildings have already been included in this grade, and the number will be increased.'

The new instruction, of November 1969, read in part as follows:

INSTRUCTION TO INVESTIGATORS

The Administration has decided, with the concurrence of the Advisory Committee, that Grade III shall be abolished from this date onwards. This will necessitate that in the newly revised lists a large number of buildings previously graded as III or about to be included in that grade will have to be made Grade II. Those buildings which cannot qualify for the Statutory List but which would have been made Grade III prior to the abolition of that grade should still be entered on the list, described and marked on the map, but no grade should be entered against them in column 2 on form HB30. These will form a Supplementary Local list sent to the Local Authority in an unofficial manner.

At the present time Grade III buildings could be held to fall into the following twelve categories:

In the country :

1 Small cottages of timber-framed construction dating from before about 1700 which have hitherto been thought to be too modest to be worth Grade II.
2 Farmhouses of the same period which have been refaced with other materials such as brick, tile-hanging or weather boarding and in so doing have lost much of their original character but show some trace of their ancient origin in individual features such as a chimney.
3 C18 or early C19 houses of very plain character with few special features.
4 Manor houses or mansions, mainly of C18 date, so much altered in the C19 as to have more the character of that date than of their original period.

In towns :

5 Buildings of any period whose ground floor has been converted into a shop but whose upper portion is not sufficiently impressive on its own to justify statutory listing.
6 Timber-framed buildings so greatly altered as to appear largley C19 but nevertheless clearly of ancient origin.
7 Plain or very modest C18 or early C19 houses.
8 The last productions of the Georgian tradition, namely very late buildings of 1830-40.
9 C19 buildings which have been badly mutilated.
10 C19 buildings that group with other statutorily listed C19 buildings but are of definitely poorer quality.
11 Buildings in a planned estate or group which have survived intact but are of modest quality.

In both towns and villages :

12 Buildings in informal groups of mixed quality in which the groups were not hitherto thought so important that it was essential for each item to be listed statutorily.
13 Curiosities.

It has been decided by the Advisory Committee that all Grade III buildings which come within the above categories 1, 2, 6, 11, 12, or 13 should automatically be upgraded to II on revision of the lists. The buildings in the other categories would be treated on their merits. Some would be upgraded and others left on the Supplementary Local list. Categories 8 and 11 might overlap a little, thereby allowing a certain latitude . . .

4 November 1969   Chief Investigator

At the public enquiry of autumn 1970 into the proposed new government building in Whitehall, a witness from the Department of the Environment offered a third description of Grade I buildings: 'Buildings of such great architectural or historic interest that they could not be demolished apart from the most exceptional circumstances.'

The formulation in use in 1968 implied, as the attentive reader will have noticed, that though 'public utility schemes' should not be allowed to cause the demolition of Grade I buildings, private development might. This was inadvertent.

Appendix 2

MAGDALENE COLLEGE, CAMBRIDGE: CONVERSION OF EXISTING BUILDINGS TO COLLEGE USE 1953-70

Contract	Existing use	Converted use	Cost £ (incl. 10% fees)
1953 Mallory Cottages 4-11 (20 Magdalene Street)	Ground floor extension to shop, old stables and lofts	2 roomed sets for 8 students incl. baths, etc.	8,529
1954 Mallory Court 12-17	Decorators' store and garage	2 roomed sets for 6 students incl. baths, etc.	6,827
1954 J & H Staircases (25 Magdalene Street)	House over shop, existing sub-standard college rooms	2 roomed sets for 7 students incl. baths, etc. 3 bedsitting rooms Lock-up shop and store	917 1,571 1,768
1954 L Staircase (29 Magdalene Street) 1956 Further work	House over shop	3 bedsitting rooms, bath, etc. Lock-up shop and store	1,180 875

Contract	Existing use	Converted use	Cost £ (incl. 10% fees)
1955 K Staircase (26-28 Magdalene Street)	3 shops with living accommodation over	2 Lock-up shops with stores, etc. 2 roomed sets for 6 students incl. baths, etc., porter's lodge	5,793
1955 N Staircase (31 Magdalene Street)	Shop, derelict boat-yard and office, sub-standard flat over	Office, 2 roomed sets for 4 students incl. baths, etc. 1 bedsitting room Lock-up shop and store	929 1,557 286
1955 J Staircase (23/24 Magdalene Street)	2 shops with living accommodation over	2 roomed set for 1 student 1 bedsitting room 2 lock-up shops with stores, etc.	3,280
1956 J Staircase (22 Magdalene Street)	Shop with living accommodation over	2 bedsitting rooms, bathroom etc. Lock-up shop and stores	2,613
1956 M Staircase (Bullens Cottage)	Derelict cottage	2 roomed sets for 2 students incl. bath, etc. 1 bedsitting room	2,571
1958 12-17 Mallory Cottages	Some existing college rooms and college servants house (little alteration required)	2 roomed sets for 5 students incl. baths, etc.	476

Contract	Existing use	Converted use	Cost £ (incl. 10% fees)
1958 18-20 Mallory Cottages	Decoration only required	2 roomed sets for 2 students incl. bath 1 bedsitting room	
1965 Buckingham Court 1-4 (Tan Yard Cottages)	Sub-standard former almshouses—six households	2 roomed sets for 8 students incl. baths, etc.	16,200
1965 10-18 Northampton Street	9 sub-standard houses	3 houses (generally 2 into 1) Offices for Lucy Cavendish College	19,847
1966 19 Northampton Street	Sub-standard house	Rehabilitated one house	5,346
1968 8-9 Northampton Street	Shop and taxi office	Rehabilitated one house	5,841
1970 21-25 Mallory Cottages (17a Magdalene Street)	Lodging house	2 roomed sets for 5 students incl. baths, etc.	4,807

Appendix 3

A list of relevant bodies and organisations

Ancient Monuments Society (voluntary society)
12 Edwardes Square
London W8

Civic Trust
(voluntary society, grouping urban amenity societies)
17 Carlton House Terrace
London SW1

Council for British Archaeology
(learned and academic society)
8 St Andrews Place
Regent's Park
London NW1

Council for the Protection of Rural England
(voluntary society with county branches)
4 Hobart Place
London SW1

Georgian Group (voluntary society)
2 Chester Street
London SW1

Historic Buildings Bureau
(specialist house agency run by Government)
2 Marsham Street
London SW1

Historic Buildings Council for England (statutory body)
25 Savile Row
London W1

217

National Trust (independent body)
42 Queen Anne's Gate
London SW1

Royal Commission on Historical Monuments
(statutory body)
Fielden House,
10 Great College Street
London SW1

Royal Fine Arts Commission (statutory body)
2 Carlton Gardens
London SW1

Society for the Protection of Ancient Buildings
(voluntary society)
55 Great Ormond Street
London WC1

Society of Antiquaries (learned society)
Burlington House
Piccadilly
London W1

Victorian Society (voluntary society)
12 Magnolia Wharf
Strand-on-the-Green
London W4

Index

INDEX

Abercrombie, Lord, 141
Action Areas, 74, *see also* Development Planning
Advisory Council on Noise, 74
Ancient Monuments Consolidation Bill (1912), 34-8, 67; Acts (1913) 34-8; (1931), 38; (1933), 39
Ancient Monuments Protection Act (1882), 29-31, 32, 34, 36, 37
Ancient Monuments Society, 83, 217
Anthropological Society, 22
Appeal Planning Ltd, 139-40
Aubrey, John, 15-16, 31; preservation style, 120-21, 199, 201, 203
Avebury, Wiltshire, 16, 22, 30
Avebury, Lord, *see* Lubbock, Sir John
Avignon, 55-61

Bampton Property Group Ltd, 146-48, 150, 152-53
Bath, 54; Beaufort Square, 131-54, 198; City Council, 91, 131-53; Municipal Charities, 132, 145; Preservation Trust, 132-53; Town Clerk, 136 37, 141-53; *see also* Four Towns Reports and Studies
Bath and Wilts Chronicle, 134, 138, 151
Bath Evening Chronicle, 136, 138, 141, 142
Beauchamp, 7th Earl, 34, 35
Beazer, C. H. & Sons Ltd, Bath, 142, 145
Bedford, 13th Duke of, 88
Betjeman, Sir John, 52, 106
British Tourist and Holidays Association, 88-89
Brown, George, MP, 72
Buchanan, Professor Colin, 68, 91
Buck, H. J., 81

Building Preservation Notice, 84, 122; Order, 75-78, 84
Bulmer Thomas, Ivor, MP, 101
Burghclere, Lord, 31, 34
Burrows, G. S., 68, 91

Cambridge, Magdalene College, 202-13, 213-15; St John's College, 54
Camden Society, 18
Carter, John, *Gentleman's Magazine*, 17
Central Pollution Control Unit, 74
Channon, Paul, MP, 48, 84
Chester *see* Four Towns Reports
Chesterton, Elizabeth, 69
Chichester *see* Four Towns Reports
Church Assembly, 102
Churches, preservation of, 100, 101-03
Civic Amenities Act (1967), 65, 196
Civic Trust, 65, 104, 106, 122, 128, 201, 217; pamphlets, 108, 119; at York, 121, 201
Clarke, Geoffrey, architect, 202-03
Commissioners of Works, 34, 36, 39, 45
Conservation Areas, 65-68, 83
Conservation Bill (1971), 67
Cowley, John, 145
Council for British Archaeology, 83, 136, 217
Council for the Preservation of Rural England, 40
Council for the Protection of Rural England, 217
Crisp's Estate Agency, Bath, 145-46
Cripps, Sir Stafford, 40
Crosby, Theo, architect, 71
Crossman, Richard, MP, 65, 71, 73, 103, 105; and conference on historic towns, 50-51, 68

221

Democracy 36